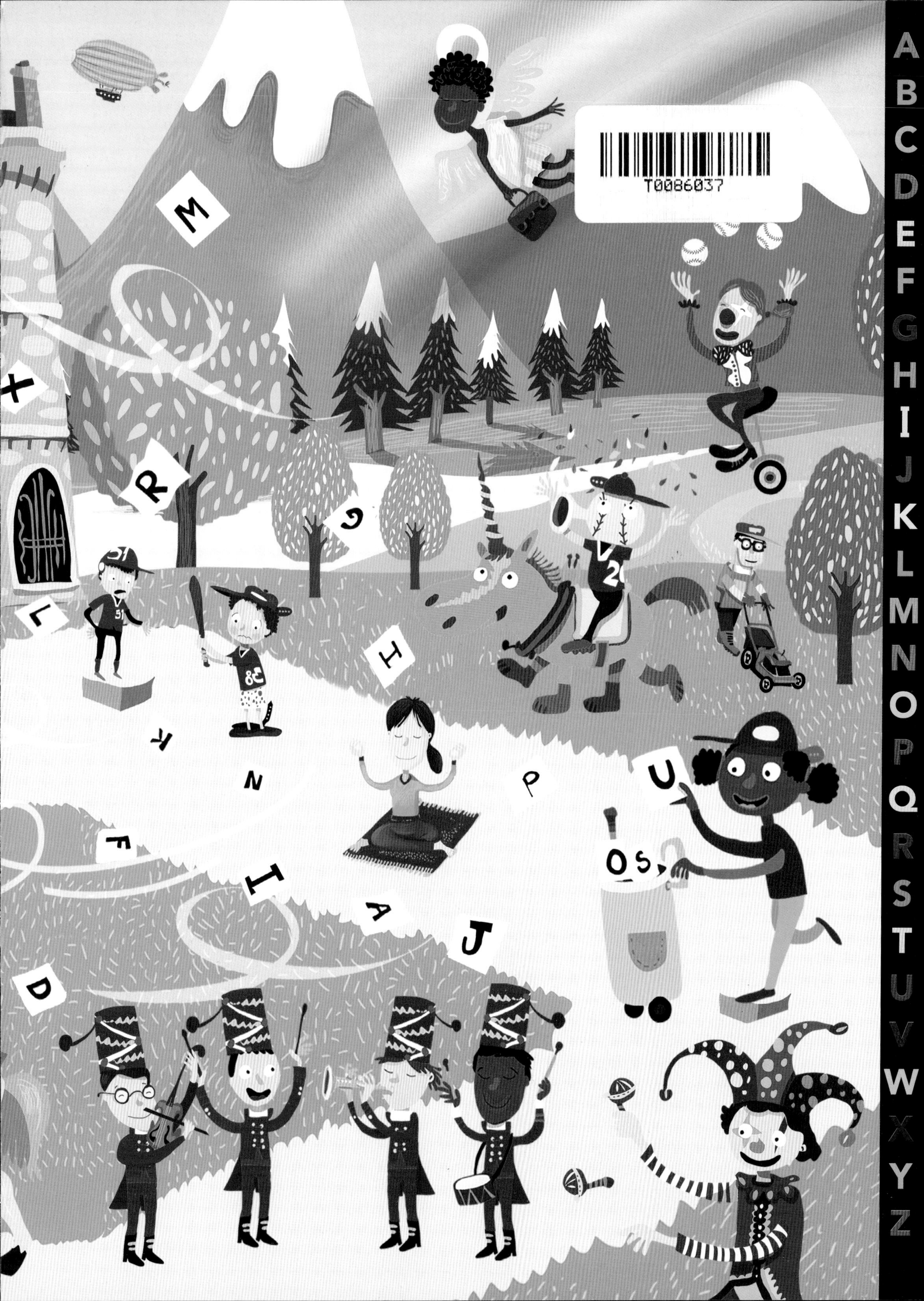
ABCDEFGHIJKLMNOPQRSTUVWXYZ

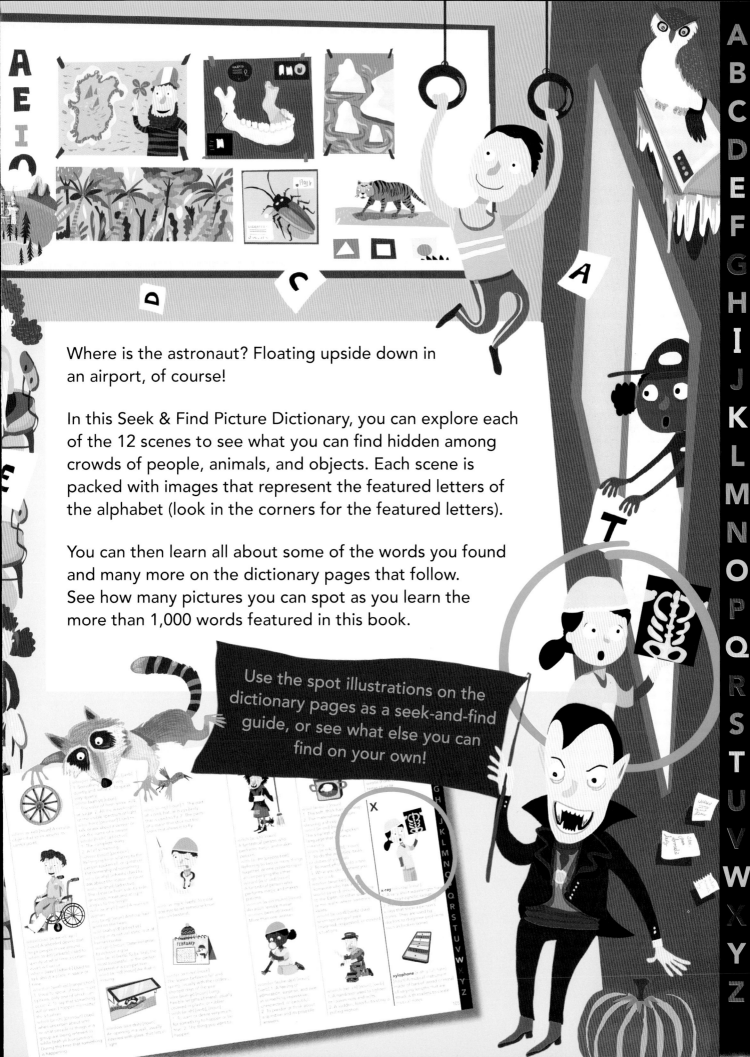

Where is the astronaut? Floating upside down in an airport, of course!

In this Seek & Find Picture Dictionary, you can explore each of the 12 scenes to see what you can find hidden among crowds of people, animals, and objects. Each scene is packed with images that represent the featured letters of the alphabet (look in the corners for the featured letters).

You can then learn all about some of the words you found and many more on the dictionary pages that follow. See how many pictures you can spot as you learn the more than 1,000 words featured in this book.

Use the spot illustrations on the dictionary pages as a seek-and-find guide, or see what else you can find on your own!

How do you say *astronaut*? Look no further than the pronunciation guide next to each word.

Our pronunciations are designed to help young readers break down words into individual sounds. Phonemic awareness, or the ability to break words down into individual sounds, is an essential skill for emergent readers.

The pronunciations given in this book are written phonetically to support children as they sound out each word.

For example, the word *please* is broken down into phonemes: pl-eez.

Note: In words with a double o sound, as in book (b-*oo*-k), "*oo*" is in italics to differentiate its sound from the other oo sound, as in school (sk-ool).

In addition, each word has a part of speech listed to help readers better understand how words are used in a grammatical sense. This supports skills such as sentence structure and writing. Definitions are also written in kid-friendly language to support comprehension.

What skills will you learn with this Seek & Find Picture Dictionary? ➡️

- **Common Phonics Patterns**
- **Phonemic Awareness**
- **Spelling**
- Alphabetic Order
- **Vocabulary Families**
- **Recognition and Prediction**
- Object Identification
- **Synonyms**
- Antonyms

B

A

a (ay) [noun] 1. The first letter of the English alphabet.
2. A vowel.

able (ay-bl) [adjective] Having the skill or resources to do something.

about (uh-bowt) [preposition] 1. Concerning or with regard to. 2. Near or close to.

above (uh-buv) [adverb] In a higher place.

accident (ak-si-dent) [noun] An undesirable and unintended happening.

acrobat (ak-roh-bat) [noun] An entertainer who performs difficult physical feats, jumps, and walks on their hands.

across (uh-kraws) [preposition] From one side to the opposite side.

act (akt) [noun], [verb] 1. Anything done, being done, or to be done. 2. To do or behave in a particular way.

add (ad) [verb] To join two or more things for a greater total.

address (ah-dres) [noun], [verb] 1. Details identifying a location, such as where someone lives or works: school address, home address, etc. 2. To communicate directly to someone.

adult (uh-dult) [noun] A fully grown person or animal.

aerosol can (eh-ruh-sahl k-an) [noun] A can that sprays a pressurized gas.

afraid (uh-frayd) [adjective] Worried or frightened by something or that something bad may happen.

after (af-tur) [preposition] Immediately following someone or something else.

again (uh-gen) [adverb] When something happens once more.

against (uh-gehnst) [preposition] 1. In disagreement with. 2. Competing with. 3. Something touching another surface.

age (ay-j) [noun], [verb] 1. How old something is as measured in time. 2. The process of getting older.

ago (uh-go) [adverb] Before the present time.

agree (uh-gree) [verb] To share the same opinion, idea, or decision.

ahead (uh-hed) [adverb] In front of someone or something.

air (ayr) [noun] A mixture of invisible gases that we breathe.

airplane (ayr-playn) [noun] A winged vehicle that travels through the sky.

airport (ayr-port) [noun] A place where airplanes take off and land, picking up and dropping off cargo and passengers.

alarm (uh-lahrm) [noun] 1. A state of panic. 2. A sound meant to alert.

alien (ay-lee-en) [noun] A being from another world in outer space.

alive (uh-lahyv) [adjective] Having life.

all (awl) [adjective] The whole amount of something.

alligator (al-uh-g-ay-tur) [noun] A large reptile with scales and sharp teeth that lives in or near lakes or ponds.

allow (uh-laow) [verb] 1. To let someone do something. 2. To let something happen.

alphabet (al-fuh-bet) [noun] A collection of letters in a specific order, each having a unique sound used to make words.

also (awl-so) [adverb] In addition to something previously mentioned.

always (awl-wayz) [adverb] The same at all times.

am (aem) [verb] To be or to do when referring to yourself.

ambulance (aem-byoo-lens) [noun] A vehicle for bringing sick or injured people to the hospital in an emergency.

among (uh-mung) [preposition] In the middle or midst of.

an (aen) [indefinite article] Used when the word after it begins with a vowel sound.

anchor (ayn-ker) [noun], [verb] 1. A heavy object thrown off of a boat, connected by a chain, to stop the boat from moving. 2. To hold in place.

and (aend) [conjunction] Joins words together in a phrase.

angel (ayn-jel) [noun] A figure often shown with a halo and wings.

anger (ayng-gur) [noun] A strong feeling of displeasure about something or someone.

angry (ayng-gree) [adjective] Feeling mad.

animal (aen-uh-muhl) [noun] Living creatures, such as mammals, insects, reptiles, and birds.

answer (aen-sur) [noun] A response to a question.

ant (aent) [noun] A small insect that creates pathways underground and can carry large loads.

anteater (aent-ee-tur) [noun] An animal with a long tongue that eats ants.

antelope (aent-uh-lohp) [noun] An animal from Africa and Asia with antlers.

antenna (aen-ten-uh) [noun] 1. A piece of metal that takes in and sends out signals, typically found on cars or radios. 2. Part of an insect or crustacean that allows them to feel what is around them.

anthill (aent-h-ill) [noun] A mound of dirt made by an ant that leads to colonies.

any (en-ee) [determiner] One or more of something taken at random.

anyone (en-ee-wuhn) [pronoun] Referring to any person.

appear (uh-peer) [verb] To show up or come into sight.

apple (ah-pull) [noun] A firm red, yellow, or green round fruit that grows on trees, is white inside, and has seeds.

apron (ay-pruhn) [noun] A piece of clothing worn to protect clothes from getting dirty in the kitchen.

aqualung (ah-kwuh-luhng) [noun] A device that allows a person to breathe underwater.

A B C D E F G H I J K L M N O P Q R S T U V W X Y Z

13

arc (ahr-k) [noun] Something arched or curved.

are (ahr) [verb] The present tense and plural of the word *be*.

area (air-ee-uh) [noun] 1. A particular part of someplace. 2. The size of a space or surface.

arm (ahrm) [noun] The body part between a person's shoulder and wrist.

armadillo (ahrm-uh-dil-low) [noun] An animal with an armor-like shell that can roll into a ball.

armchair (ahrm-chayr) [noun] A chair with elevated pieces to rest your arms on.

arrange (uh-raynj) [verb] To organize or move things around in a particular order.

arrive (uh-rahyv) [verb] To get to a specific place or time.

art (ahrt) [noun] The expression of feelings or ideas: painting, drawing, sculpting, dance, music, etc.

artichoke (ahr-ti-chohk) [noun] A green vegetable that looks like a closed flower.

artist (ahr-tist) [noun] A person who creates art.

as (az) [adverb] Used when you are comparing two things.

ask (a-sk) [verb] To request information or help.

astronaut (a-stroh-nawt) [noun] A person who travels to outer space.

at (a-t) [preposition] Used to say where or when something happens.

athlete (ath-leet) [noun] A person who is skilled in sports.

atom (at-um) [noun] The smallest part of an element.

awake (uh-wayk) [verb], [adjective] 1. To arouse from sleep. 2. Not sleeping.

ax (aks) [noun] A tool with a steel blade used to chop wood.

B

baby (bay-bee) [noun] A very young child, especially one recently born.

back (b-ak) [noun], [adverb] 1. The rear part of a human torso. 2. Toward the rear. 3. To a place where something came from.

backpack (bak-pak) [noun] A bag with straps so that you can hang it on your back.

bad (b-ad) [adjective] 1. Not good in any way. 2. Poor quality.

badge (b-aj) [noun]
1. A token earned, often for an achievement. 2. A mark or symbol.

ball (bawl) [noun] A round or nearly round object, often filled with air and used in games.
balloon (buh-loon) [noun] A small rubber bag that expands when inflated and is used as a toy or decoration.

banana (buh-nan-uh) [noun] A sweet, yellow fruit with a peel that grows in the tropics.
band (band) [noun], [verb]
1. A group of people who make music together. 2. To unite or come together.
bank (bangk) [noun] 1. A place to keep money. 2. A sloped surface bordering a stream.
bar (bahr) [noun], [verb]
1. A solid material that is longer than it is wide: bar of soap, candy bar, gold bar, sandbar.
2. To block.

base (bays) [noun] 1. The four markers that runners touch in a baseball game. 2. The bottom or foundation of something.

baseball (bays-bawl) [noun]
1. A game played with two teams, a ball, and a bat. Players hit the ball and run around four bases to score. 2. The ball used in a baseball game.
basic (bay-sik) [adjective] Simple, plain.

bat (b-at) [noun] 1. A nocturnal flying mammal that sleeps upside down. 2. The stick the ball is hit with in a baseball game.
bath (b-ath) [noun] The act of washing yourself in a tub.

bath mat (b-ath m-at) [noun] An object meant to stop water from soaking the floor when somebody gets out of the bath.

bathtub (b-ath-tuhb) [noun] A structure that holds a large amount of water to allow people to wash themselves in it.
be (bee) [verb] To exist or live.

bear (bair) [noun] A large, furry mammal that lives in wooded areas and likes to eat fish and berries.
beat (beet) [verb] To win over competitors in a competition.
beauty (byoo-tee) [noun] Something or someone that pleases your senses.

bed (behd) [noun] A type of furniture for sleeping on.

bee (bee) [noun] A black-and-yellow-striped insect that pollinates flowers and produces honey.

15

been (bin) [verb] To have gone somewhere and come back.

beetle (bee-tul) [noun] An insect with a hard exoskeleton.

before (bee-for) [preposition] Earlier than or prior to.

begin (bee-gehn) [verb] To start something.

behind (bee-hind) [preposition], [adverb] In the rear or back of.

believe (bee-leev) [verb] To be certain that someone is being truthful or something is true.

bell (bel) [noun] A hollow, metal object that makes a ringing sound: church bell, doorbell, sleigh bell, etc.

belt (bel-t) [noun] A piece of clothing used to hold up pants and shorts.

beret (buh-ray) [noun] A round, flat hat associated with French culture, typically red or black, often with a tab at its center.

best (best) [adjective] The highest quality or better than all others.

better (bet-ur) [adjective] Superior quality or higher quality than some.

between (buh-tween) [preposition] 1. The space that separates two things. 2. Having something on both sides.

big (big) [adjective] Large; greater than average size.

bike (bahyk) [noun] A two-wheeled, usually pedal-powered, vehicle.

bird (b-rd) [noun] A winged and feathered creature that lays eggs.

birdhouse (brd-hows) [noun] Outdoor furniture often made of wood for birds to build nests in.

birthday (brth-day) [noun] The day you were born and the anniversary of the day you were born.

bit (bit) [noun], [verb] 1. A small piece of something. 2. The past tense of bite.

black (blak) [adjective] The dark color of coal or night.

blanket (blang-kit) [noun], [verb] 1. A large piece of soft fabric. 2. To cover something.

block (blok) [noun], [verb] 1. A solid mass of material used for building. 2. To stop something from happening.

blow (bloh) [verb], [noun] 1. Movement of a current of air. 2. A strong wind.

blue (bloo) [adjective] 1. The primary color between green and indigo. 2. The color of the sky.

board (bohrd) [noun] A long piece of thinly sawed wood.

boat (boht) [noun] A vessel for transport in water.

body (b-aw-dee) [noun] 1. All of the parts that make up a person or animal: head, hands, feet, etc. 2. A large amount of something.

bone (bohn) [noun] Hard parts that make up the skeleton of a person or animal.

book (b-oo-k) [noun] Printed pages bound together with a cover.

boot (b-oo-t) [noun] Tall footwear made to protect feet from getting wet, cold, or injured.

born (bohrn) [verb] When a human or animal comes out of their mother's body or an egg.
both (bohth) [adjective] One and the other.

bottle (bah-tul) [noun] An object used to hold liquids that has a cap or lid.
bottom (bah-tum) [noun] The lowest or deepest part of something.
bought (bawt) [verb]
1. The past tense of buy.
2. To have purchased something.
bowl (bohl) [noun] A deep, round dish or basin often used to hold liquids or food.

bowling (bohl-ing) [noun] A sport in which the goal is to knock down a set of ten pins with as few rolls of a ball as possible.

box (boks) [noun] A container or case for putting things in, often with straight sides.
boy (boi) [noun] A male child.
branch (branch) [noun] The part of a tree that grows out from the trunk and where leaves grow.

bread (bred) [noun] A food made with flour and water baked into a loaf.
break (brayk) [verb] To separate into pieces.
breakfast (brek-fust) [noun] The first meal of the day.
brick (brik) [noun] Hard blocks of building material made from baked clay.
bright (brahyt) [adjective] Radiant light shining strongly.
bring (br-ing) [verb] Taking someone or something from one place to another.
broad (brod) [adjective] Wide.
broke (brohk) [verb], [adjective]
1. The past tense of break.
2. Having no money.
brother (bruh-thur) [noun] A male with whom you share parents.
brought (brawt) [verb] The past tense of bring.
brown (brown) [adjective] The color of dirt and tree trunks.

brush (bruhsh) [noun]
1. Small bushes. 2. A tool used to paint or to untangle hair.
bubble (buh-bl) [noun] A ball of gas surrounded by a liquid that floats in air.
bug (buhg) [noun], [verb]
1. Another word for insect.
2. To annoy.
build (billd) [verb] To assemble something.

building (bill-ding) [noun] A constructed set of walls and floors that houses people and objects.
bun (buhn) [noun] A type of bread, usually round.
burn (b-r-n) [verb], [noun]
1. To produce heat and flames.
2. An injury caused by heat.
bus (buhs) [noun] A large vehicle for carrying lots of people.
busy (biz-ee) [adjective] Occupied with many activities.
but (buht) [conjunction] A word used to connect two statements when one is different than the first.
butterfly (buht-er-fly) [noun] A flying insect with big, often brightly colored wings.
buy (bahy) [verb] To purchase something with money.
by (bahy) [preposition] Indicates who or what does something or how it was done.

C

cactus (kak-tuh-s) [noun] A plant with sharp needles that grows in a dry environment that needs very little water.

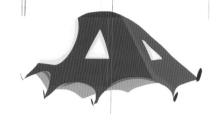

cake (k-ay-k) [noun] A food made from flour, butter, sugar, and eggs, often made in celebration of something.

calculator (kalk-yuh-lay-tr) [noun] A small electronic device used to solve mathematical problems.

calendar (kal-in-der) [noun] Pages that show months, days, and weeks for a year at a time.

call (k-aw-l) [verb] To reach out to someone with your voice, often using a phone.

came (k-ay-m) [verb]
1. The past tense of *come*.
2. To have traveled to a destination.

camel (k-am-ul) [noun] A mammal in desert regions with one or two humps that can survive without water for many days.

camera (k-am-uh-ruh) [noun] A device to record visual images: photographs or videos.

camp (k-amp) [noun], [verb]
1. A group of tents, cabins, or huts. 2. To set up a temporary shelter, such as a tent, and stay there a short while.

campfire (k-amp-f-ah-yr) [noun] A fire made out of sticks, commonly used while camping.

can (k-an) [noun] A metal container used to preserve food or drink.

canoe (k-uh-noo) [noun] A long wooden boat used in water.

cap (k-ap) [noun] A close-fitting hat.

capital (kap-i-tl) [noun]
1. An uppercase letter.
2. An important city in each state, province, or country where the main government for that area resides.

captain (kap-tin) [noun]
1. The person in charge of a boat, plane, or group of people. 2. A military rank.

car (k-ah-r) [noun] 1. A four-wheeled vehicle for carrying a small number of people. 2. Part of a train.

card (k-ah-rd) [noun] A small, thin piece of paper, plastic, or similar material on which important information is given.

cards (k-ah-rd-z) [noun] A deck of 52 rectangular pieces of paper displaying numbers and images that are used to play games.

care (k-ay-r) [verb] The act of tending to or looking after something or someone.

carpet (kah-r-pit) [noun] A floor covering made from woven material.

carrot (k-ayr-ut) [noun] An orange root vegetable that provides the body with vitamin A.
carry (k-ay-ree) [verb] To hold something in your hands or arms as you take it somewhere.

cart (k-ahr-t) [noun] A large basket with wheels used to hold and transport goods.

case (k-ay-s) [noun] 1. A type of container used to store or transport objects. 2. A particular situation or example.
cast (k-as-t) [noun], [verb] 1. Something worn to protect a broken limb. 2. To throw a fishing line into water in an attempt to catch a fish.

castaway (k-as-t-uh-way) [noun] A person who has been shipwrecked or stranded on an island away from civilization.

castle (ka-sl) [noun] A large building made to protect the people who live there; usually old and made of stone.

cat (k-at) [noun] A small, furry, four-legged mammal that purrs and is often kept as a pet.

catch (k-ach) [verb] 1. To stop and hold something that was moving, such as a ball or a criminal. 2. To see someone doing something they did not want you to see.
caterpillar (kat-r-pil-r) [noun] A small worm-like creature that turns into a butterfly.
caught (k-aw-t) [verb] The past tense of catch.
cause (k-aw-z) [verb], [noun] 1. To make something happen. 2. The person or thing that made something happen.

cave (k-ay-v) [noun] A hollowed-out part of a natural structure; can be natural or human-made.

cell (sel) [noun] The smallest unit of an organism.
cent (sent) [noun] One one-hundredth of a dollar, also known as a penny.
center (sen-tr) [noun] 1. The exact middle. 2. A place to gather for a particular purpose.
century (sen-chu-ree) [noun] One hundred years.
certain (sr-tn) [adjective] To be absolutely sure of something.

chair (ch-ay-r) [noun] A piece of furniture made for one person to sit in. Usually has a seat, a back, and four legs.
chance (ch-ans) [noun] The possibility of something happening.
change (ch-ay-nj) [noun], [verb] 1. A group of coins. 2. To transform or convert from one thing to another.
character (kayr-ik-tr) [noun] 1. The combination of features, qualities, or traits that make a person or thing special. 2. A person or animal in a story.
charge (ch-ah-rj) [noun], [verb] 1. The asking price or fee. 2. A stored amount of electrical energy. 3. To move quickly toward something in attack.
chart (ch-ah-rt) [noun] An organized representation of information; a picture or graph.
check (ch-ek) [noun], [verb] 1. A piece of paper promising payment from the bank. 2. To investigate something.

21

chef (sh-e-f) [noun] The person who cooks the menu at a restaurant.

cherry (ch-ay-ree) [noun] A small, round, often red fruit that has a pit and grows on trees.

chick (ch-ik) [noun] A baby bird.

chicken (ch-ik-en) [noun] A farm bird that lays eggs.

chief (ch-eef) [noun] 1. The person in charge of an organization. 2. The head of a tribe.

child (ch-ah-yld) [noun] A young person, not yet an adult.

children (ch-ild-ren) [noun] More than one young person.

choose (ch-oo-z) [verb] To pick from a group or selection.

chord (k-ord) [noun] 1. A combination of several musical notes played together. 2. In geometry, a straight line joining two points in a curve.

chore (ch-ohr) [noun] A task that someone has been given, often done at home.

chose (ch-ohz) [verb] The past tense of choose.

circle (sir-kul) [noun] A completely round shape.

city (sit-ee) [noun] A large town.

claim (kl-ay-m) [verb], [noun] 1. To declare that something is true. 2. A declaration of ownership of something.

clam (kl-am) [noun] An underwater shelled creature that sometimes holds pearls.

class (kl-as) [noun] 1. A group of people who learn together. 2. The room where students meet to learn. 3. A group sharing common features.

clean (kl-een) [adjective], [verb] 1. Free from marks or mess; not dirty. 2. To remove dirt or mess.

clear (kl-eer) [adjective] 1. Easy to see through. 2. Easy to understand.

climb (kl-ah-ym) [verb] Using your feet and hands to move your body up, across, or down something.

clock (kl-ok) [noun] An instrument displaying the time.

close (kl-ohz/kl-ohs) [verb], [adjective] 1. To shut something. 2. Describes something or somebody nearby.

clothes (kl-oh-thz) [noun] Items that people wear to cov and protect their bodies.

cloud (kl-owd) [noun] White ar gray masses of small drops of water floating in the sky.

clover (kl-oh-vr) [noun] A smal green plant with three leaves and in rare cases, four.

coast (k-oh-st) [noun], [verb] 1. Where the land meets the ocean. 2. Moving forward with little or no effort.

coat (k-oh-t) [noun], [verb] 1. Long-sleeved clothing worn over other clothes to protect them and keep you warm and dry. 2. To cover something.

coconut (ko-kuh-nut) [noun] A fruit with a hairy, hard exteri containing a sweet, white mea and milk on the inside that grows on palm trees.

cold (k-oh-ld) [adjective], [noun] 1. Having a low temperature. The opposite of warm. 2. A common sickness often involving a runny nose, coughing, and sneezing.

collect (k-oh-lekt) [verb] Bring together.

colony (kol-on-ee) [noun] 1. A group of people who settle or live together away from their native country. 2. A group of the same type of plant or animal living or growing together.

color (k-uh-lr) [noun], [verb] 1. Having pigment or a color. The primary colors are red, yellow, and blue. 2. To give something color.

column (kol-uh-m) [noun] A solid, upright support structure.

comb (k-oh-m) [noun] Tool used to brush hair.

come (k-uh-m) [verb] To move toward something.

comic (k-aw-mi-k) [noun] 1. A set of panels with art and dialogue meant to entertain through a story. 2. A comedian.

common (kom-uhn) [adjective] 1. Something that happens a lot. 2. Something shared by many.

company (kuhm-puh-nee) [noun] 1. A business organization. 2. Being with other people.

compare (kuhm-pay-r) [verb] To notice if things are alike or different.

complete (kuhm-pleet) [verb], [adjective] 1. To finish. 2. Nothing is missing.

condition (kuhn-dish-uhn) [noun] A state of being; how someone or something looks, acts, feels, or works.

connect (kuhn-ekt) [verb] To join or link together.

consider (kuhn-sid-r) [verb] Think about.

consonant (kon-suh-nuh-nt) [noun] The letters in the alphabet that represent consonant sounds (b, c, d, f, g, h, j, k, l, m, n, p, q, r, s, t, v, w, x, y, z).

contain (kuhn-tay-n) [verb] To hold something or to keep something under control.

continent (kon-tin-ent) [noun] One of Earth's seven main divisions of land masses.

continue (kuhn-tin-yoo) [verb] To go on after something has stopped.

control (kuhn-troh-l) [verb] The ability to make something happen the way you want.

cook (k-oo-k) [verb], [noun] 1. To prepare food for eating using heat. 2. A person who prepares food.

cool (k-ool) [adjective] A temperature that is a little cold, but not too cold.

cop (k-aw-p) [noun] Another name for a police officer; someone who is trained to uphold the law.

copy (k-aw-pee) [verb], [noun] 1. To do something the same as someone else. 2. Something that is made to be exactly like another thing.

corn (k-orn) [noun] 1. A tall plant with large, yellow seeds that grow on cobs. 2. The vegetable made from the corn plant and used for animal feed is also called corn.

corner (k-orn-r) [noun] Where two edges or lines meet.

correct (k-or-ekt) [adjective] Having no mistakes or errors.

cost (k-aw-st) [noun] The amount of money that you need to pay for something.

cotton (k-aw-tuhn) [noun]
1. A plant used to make fabric from the white hairs on its seeds. 2. The fabric made from the plant.

couch (k-ow-ch) [noun] A piece of furniture made for two or more people to sit on.

could (k-oo-d) [verb] Expressing a possibility or an ability.

count (k-ow-nt) [verb], [noun]
1. To say numbers or calculate a total (1,2,3…). 2. A nobleman.

country (k-uhn-tree) [noun]
1. An area of land ruled by its own government. 2. A term for the land outside of cities and towns, away from built-up populations; a rural area.

course (k-or-s) [noun] The way something is planned to go or the way something does happen.

cover (k-uh-vr) [verb], [noun]
1. To provide shelter.
2. Something that is put on top of something else to protect it.

cow (kow) [noun] A large female farm animal that produces milk.

crayon (kray-awn) [noun]
A colored stick of wax used for art.

crease (kr-ee-s) [noun] A fold in something.

create (kr-ee-ay-t) [verb]
To invent, build, or make something.

crib (kr-ib) [noun] A small bed designed for babies to keep them safe while sleeping.

crocodile (krok-uh-dah-yl) [noun] A large, dangerous reptile with many sharp teeth and a powerful tail that lives in hot, wet environments.

crook (kr-oo-k) [noun]
A criminal or someone who has broken the law.

crop (krop) [noun] Plants, vegetables, or fruits grown to be eaten or utilized to make materials.

cross (kros) [verb] To mix two things or intersect.

crowd (kr-owd) [noun] A large group of people gathered together.

crown (kr-own) [noun]
A headpiece worn by a king or queen made of gold and jewels.

cruise (k-r-ooz) [noun]
A luxury vacation on a large ship.

cry (kr-ah-y) [verb], [noun]
1. To have tears come from your eyes, usually because you are unhappy or hurt. 2. A loud noise made by a person or animal.

cup (k-up) [noun] A small container that holds liquid for drinking, sometimes with a handle.

current (kur-ent) [noun], [adjective] 1. A flow of electricity or water. 2. Meaning something exists or is happening right now.

cut (kut) [verb] 1. To make a hole or mark in something. 2. To make something smaller.

D

dad (dad) [noun] 1. Father. 2. A man who has a child.

daisy (day-zee) [noun] A white flower with a yellow center.

damp (damp) [adjective] Slightly wet.

dance (dan-s) [verb], [noun]
1. Rhythmic movement to music. 2. The act or art of dancing.

dandelion (dan-duh-l-ah-y-un) [noun] A flower made of seeds that are spread by the wind.
danger (dayn-jer) [noun] The possibility that something bad will happen.
dark (d-ah-rk) [adjective]
1. No light. 2. Black or slightly black.
dash (d-ash) [verb] To run quickly for a short period of time.
date (day-t) [noun]
1. A particular day of the month or year. 2. An appointment to meet. 3. The fruit of a palm tree.
daughter (daw-ter) [noun] Someone's female child.
day (day) [noun]
1. The opposite of night.
2. A twenty-four-hour period.
deal (deel) [noun], [verb]
1. An arrangement or agreement. 2. To pass out playing cards.
dear (deer) [noun], [adjective] A term that is used when speaking to someone you care for.
decide (dis-ah-yd) [verb] To think about possibilities and make a choice.

decimal (des-im-uhl) [noun], [adjective] 1. Numbers less than one and greater than zero. 2. The way a decimal number is expressed using a decimal point: .001, tenths, hundredths, thousandths.
deck (dek) [noun] 1. The main floor of a ship. 2. A flat wooden structure adjoined to a house. 3. A pack of playing cards.
deep (deep) [adjective] A distance measuring far down from the top or far into something from the outside.

deer (deer) [noun] A woodland animal that sometimes has antlers, lives in forests, and is usually very timid.
degree (dig-ree) [noun]
1. A unit for measuring temperature. 2. A course of study at university or college.
dentist (den-tist) [noun] A doctor for your teeth.
depend (dip-end) [verb]
1. To trust or have confidence in something or someone.
2. To rely on.
describe (disk-rah-yb) [verb] To give an account or details of something or someone.
desert (dez-ert) [noun] A hot, dry area of land with very little rainfall or plants, except for cactus.
design (diz-ah-yn) [verb] To draw, plan, or create something for a specific purpose or intent.

desk (desk) [noun] A piece of furniture, such as a table, with a large, flat surface designed for doing work on.
determine (dit-er-min) [verb] To consider the facts to make a decision.
develop (div-el-up) [verb] To grow through a process of growth or change.

diamond (dah-y-mund) [noun]
1. Crystallized carbon forming a very hard stone; considered a valuable gem.
2. A four-cornered shape with no right angles.
dictionary (dik-shun-air-ee) [noun] An organized list of words in alphabetical order that gives meanings for each word and explains how to say them.
did (did) [verb] The past tense of *do*.
differ (dif-er) [verb] To be unlike others or disagree in some way.
different (dif-er-unt) [adjective]
1. Not the same. 2. Unlike others.

25

difficult (dif-ik-alt) [adjective]
1. Hard to do or understand.
2. Hard to deal with.
dig (dig) [verb] 1. To create a hole by removing earth.
2. To uncover or search for something.
dinner (din-er) [noun] A meal eaten in the evening.
direct (der-ekt) [verb]
1. To guide an activity.
2. To request or instruct with authority.

dirty (der-tee) [adjective] Not clean.
discover (dis-kuv-er) [verb] To find someone or something.
discuss (dis-kus) [verb] To talk about ideas or opinions with others.
dish (dish) [noun] A shallow bowl or a plate.
distant (dist-unt) [adjective]
1. Far away in space or time.
2. Unfriendly or unconnected.

diver (d-ah-y-ver) [noun] Someone who explores underwater using an oxygen tank.
divide (div-ah-yd) [verb], [noun]
1. To separate. 2. High ground between two rivers.

division (div-iz-yun) [noun] A separation of something into two or more parts, as in math.
do (doo) [verb] To perform, to execute, or to accomplish something.

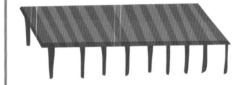

dock (d-aw-k) [noun] A structure that extends into the water where boats can load, unload, or be tied up.

doctor (dok-ter) [noun] A medical professional who helps people stay healthy and takes care of them when they are sick.
does (duz) [verb] The present tense of *do*.

dog (d-aw-g) [noun] A furry, domestic animal with four legs and a tail that is closely related to the gray wolf.

doll (d-awl) [noun] A child's toy that looks like a baby or a small person.

dollar (d-awl-er) [noun] A basic unit of money representing one hundred pennies. Used in Canada, Australia, and the United States.

dolphin (d-awl-fin) [noun] An intelligent mammal that lives in the sea.
done (d-un) [verb], [adjective]
1. The past tense of do.
2. Completed.

door (d-or) [noun] The barrier that you open to enter or exit somewhere or something: a car door, a front door, a sliding door, etc.

double (d-uh-bl) [adjective], [noun] 1. To make or become twice as much. 2. Getting to second base with one hit in a baseball game.

down (d-ow-n) [adverb], [noun] 1. Toward the bottom. 2. The opposite of up. 3. A covering of soft, fluffy feathers.

dragonfly (dra-gun-fl-ah-y) [noun] An insect that can fly straight up and down and hover, with two sets of transparent wings.

draw (dr-aw) [verb], [noun] 1. To create a picture by making lines or marks. 2. A tied score.

drawbridge (dr-aw-b-ri-j) [noun] A mechanism that can lower and raise itself to allow people to cross a body of water. The bridge will raise to either disallow people to cross or to allow large ships to pass through.

dream (dr-eem) [noun] Thoughts, feelings, images, and scenarios your mind creates during sleep.

dress (dr-es) [noun], [verb] 1. An article of clothing combining a skirt and top. 2. To put your clothes on.

drink (dr-ing-k) [verb], [noun] 1. To swallow liquid. 2. A liquid that you drink.

drip (dr-ip) [verb] When a small amount of liquid falls.

drive (dr-ah-yv) [verb] To navigate the movement of a vehicle.

drop (dr-op) [verb] 1. To stop holding something so that it falls. 2. To fall to a lower level or amount.

drum (dr-um) [noun] A musical instrument with a thin layer of material stretched over the top that is beaten with a hand or stick to make music.

dry (dr-ah-y) [adjective], [verb] 1. Free or nearly free of water. 2. To remove the water from something.

duck (duk) [noun], [verb] 1. An aquatic bird with webbed feet. 2. To drop down suddenly.

dune buggy (d-oo-n b-uh-gee) [noun] A vehicle that is made to travel over sand.

during (der-ing) [preposition] From the beginning to the end of a period of time.

X
Y

27

E

each (eech) [adjective] Every one of two or more things.

eagle (ee-gl) [noun] Large, soaring bird of prey with a sharp beak and long talons.

ear (eer) [noun] The organ of hearing and balance in humans and other vertebrates. The external part of the organ is also called the ear.

early (ur-lee) [adjective] Happening or done before the expected time.

Earth (ur-th) [noun]
1. The planet we live on.
2. One of the eight planets in our solar system.

ease (eez) [noun] Absence of difficulty or effort.

easel (ee-zul) [noun] A stand an artist uses to hold their painting while they paint.

east (ee-st) [noun] 1. One of four cardinal directions.
2. The direction the sun rises.

eat (eet) [verb] To put food into your mouth and chew and swallow it.

echo (ek-o) [noun] A series of sounds caused by the reflection of sound waves from a surface back to the listener.

eclipse (i-kl-ip-s) [noun] An event when the moon is aligned with the sun. The Earth moves in between the sun and crosses in front of the moon.

edge (ej) [noun] The outside limit of an object, area, or surface.

effect (if-ekt) [noun] A change that is a result of an action or cause.

egg (eg) [noun] An oval object laid by a female bird, reptile, or fish.

eggplant (eg- pl-ant) [noun] A purple, starchy, curved vegetable with a green top.

eight (ay-t) [noun] A number after seven and before nine.

either (ee-ther) [adjective] One or the other of two people or things.

electric (il-ek-trik) [adjective] Charged with or producing electricity.

electrician (il-ek-tri-shun) [noun] A worker who installs, maintains, or repairs electrical equipment, such as appliances.

electricity (il-ek-tris-it-ee) [noun] 1. A form of energy.
2. The supply of electric current to a house or other building.

element (el-uh-ment) [noun]
A part or aspect of something.

elephant (el-uh-fen-t) [noun]
A large, gray mammal with a trunk and two tusks.

elevator (el-uh-vay-ter) [noun]
A mechanical device that allows people to travel between floors of a building.

elf (el-f) [noun] A fantasy creature with pointed ears, often associated with Santa Claus.

else (el-s) [adverb] Used to talk about a different person, place, or thing.

e-mail (ee-may-l) [noun] Stands for "electronic mail" and refers to a message sent online through electronic devices.

emergency (ee-mer-jun-see) [noun] An urgent need for help or an unexpected situation that must be dealt with right away.

empty (emp-tee) [adjective] Having nothing inside.

encyclopedia (en-sah-y-klopee-dee-ah) [noun] A reference book that is full of detailed information about many different subjects, usually arranged alphabetically.

end (end) [noun] 1. The last part of something. 2. The furthest point from the beginning. 3. When something is finished.

enemy (en-em-ee) [noun] Someone who opposes you.

energy (en-er-jee) [noun] 1. Physical and mental strength that makes you able to do things. 2. Power that is used to provide heat and electricity.

engine (en-jin) [noun] The part of a vehicle that produces the power to make it move.

enough (ee-nuf) [adverb] An amount equal to what is needed.

enter (en-ter) [verb] To come or go into a place.

equal (ee-kwul) [adjective] Two or more things that are the same in size, number, or amount.

equate (ee-kw-ait) [verb] To make or treat something as equal to another thing.

equator (ee-kw-ait-or) [noun] An imaginary circle around the middle of the Earth that is exactly the same distance from both the South and North poles.

escalator (es-ku-lay-ter) [noun] A power-driven set of moving stairs to transport people between floors of a building.

escape (es-kay-p) [verb] To get away from or avoid a dangerous or bad situation.

especially (esp-esh-uhl-ee) [adverb] To specify that something is important or that something is unusual.

even (ee-vun) [adjective] 1. Equal in size or amount. 2. Something that is smooth and level.

evening (eev-ning) [noun] The early part of night and at the end of the day.

event (ee-vent) [noun] Something that happens that usually is important or unusual.

ever (ev-er) [adverb] 1. At any time. 2. Always.

every (ev-er-ee) [adjective] 1. All of the people or things, or all of the parts of something. 2. How often something occurs.

exact (eg-zakt) [adjective], [verb] 1. Completely correct in every detail. 2. To demand and get something by force.

example (eg-zam-pl) [noun] 1. A part of something that shows what the whole is like. 2. A problem to be solved to show how a rule works.

excavator (eks-ku-vay-ter) [noun] A machine used to dig up earth.

excellent (eks-uhl-int) [adjective] Extremely good or of a very high quality.

except (eks-ept) [preposition] A word that is used to show the only thing, person, action, or situation about which a statement is NOT true.

excited (eks-sah-y-tid) [adjective] Happy, interested, or hopeful about a situation that will or might happen.

exercise (eks-er-sah-yz) [noun], [verb] 1. Physical activity. 2. To use a power or right that you have.

exercise bike (eks-er-sah-yz b-ah-yk) [noun] A stationary bicycle used to exercise.

exhibit (ek-sib-it) [verb] To showcase the work of someone.

expect (eks-pekt) [verb] To think that something will happen because it seems likely or has been planned.

experience (ek-speer-ee-uhn-s) [noun] 1. Knowledge or skill that you gain by doing something. 2. Something that someone has done or lived through.

experiment (ek-spair-uh-ment) [noun], [verb] 1. A scientific test done to prove or disprove an idea. 2. A process in which you test a new idea or method to see if it is useful or effective.

explain (eks-play-n) [verb] 1. To tell someone something in a clear way to help them understand. 2. To give a reason for something.

explore (eks-pl-or) [verb] 1. To travel around or go into an area for discovery or adventure. 2. To discuss or think about something. 3. To look for something.

extinct (eks-tink-t) [adjective] No longer active or no longer existing.

extra (eks-tr-uh) [adjective] More than the usual amount.

eye (ah-y) [noun] The organ that allows you to see.

F

face (f-ay-s) [noun] The front part of your head where your eyes, nose, and mouth are.

fact (f-akt) [noun] Something that is known to be true.

factory (fa-k-tuh-ree) [noun] A building where people or machines make things, typically with the use of assembly lines.

fair (f-ay-r) [noun], [adjective]
1. An exhibition, usually with rides and competitions.
2. Without favoritism.
3. Neither excellent nor poor.

fairy (fay-ree) [noun] A small fantasy being who has wings and is considered magical.

fall (f-aw-l) [noun], [verb]
1. The season before winter when leaves fall from the trees; autumn. 2. To move or drop down to the ground without intending to.

family (fam-il-ee) [noun]
1. A group of people who are related to each other: mother, father, children, etc.
2. A social group different from but considered equal to a traditional family.

famous (f-ay-mus) [adjective] Known by many people in many places; often admired.

fang (f-an-g) [noun] A sharp tooth.

far (f-ah-r) [adverb] A long distance away.

farm (f-ah-rm) [noun] An area of land used for growing crops or raising animals.

farmer (f-ah-rm-er) [noun] Someone who owns or manages a farm.

fast (f-ast) [adjective] Moving quickly or in a short period of time.

father (f-ah-th-er) [noun]
1. Dad. 2. A male parent.

favor (f-ay-ver) [noun]
1. Something that you do for someone in order to be kind or to help them. 2. A small gift given at a party.

favorite (f-ay-ver-it) [adjective] The one you like the most.

fear (f-eer) [noun] What you feel when you are worried or scared that something bad is going to happen.

feather (f-eth-er) [noun] A fine, soft covering on a bird's body that helps keep them warm and dry and helps them fly.

feed (f-eed) [verb] To give food to a person or animal.

feel (f-eel) [verb] To experience emotions or physical sensations.

feet (f-eet) [noun] The plural of the word foot.

fell (f-el) [verb] The past tense of fall.

felt (f-elt) [verb], [noun]
1. The past tense of feel.
2. A soft, flat material made from wool.

fence (f-ens) [noun]
1. A wooden or metal structure surrounding an area of land.
2. A sword-fighting sport.

few (f-yoo) [adjective]
1. A small number. 2. Not many.

field (f-eel-d) [noun]
1. A large, open area of land.
2. A subject area or specialty.

fierce (f-eer-s) [adjective] Aggressive intent or determination.

fig (f-ig) [noun] A pear-shaped, small, soft, sweet fruit.

fight (f-ah-yt) [noun], [verb]
1. An argument or disagreement. 2. To struggle against another in combat.

figure (fig-yur) [noun]
1. A number or amount.
2. A famous or important person. 3. The outline or shape of something.

fill (f-il) [verb] To put enough of something into a container so that it is full.

final (f-ah-y-nl) [adjective]
1. Completed. 2. Not to be changed or undone.

find (f-ah-y-nd) [verb]
To discover something by accident or because you were looking for it.

fine (f-ah-y-n) [adjective]
1. Satisfactory or acceptable.
2. Very thin or delicate.

finger (f-ing-ger) [noun]
Part of your hand. One of the four long, jointed divisions at the end of your hand, not including the thumb.

finish (fin-ish) [verb], [noun]
1. To complete an event, activity, or time period.
2. The end of something.

fire (f-ah-yr) [noun] Burning material that produces flames.

firefighter (f-ah-yr-f-ah-yt-er) [noun] A person whose job it is to put out fires.

first (f-er-st) [adjective] Coming before all others.

fish (f-ish) [noun] A type of animal that lives in water, typically has fins and scales, and breathes through gills.

fist (f-ist) [noun] A hand with its fingers curled together in a ball.

fit (f-it) [adjective], [verb]
1. Healthy or in good physical condition. 2. To be the right size or shape.

five (f-ah-y-v) [noun] A whole number between four and six.

fix (f-ix) [verb] To repair something that was broken.

flag (fl-ag) [noun] A piece of cloth with colors, patterns, or imagery representing an organization, country, or state.

flame (fl-ay-m) [noun] A part of a fire.

flat (fl-at) [adjective]
A horizontal, level, smooth surface.

floor (fl-or) [noun] The part of a building that you walk on.

flow (fl-oh) [verb] To move in a smooth, steady motion.

flower (fl-ow-er) [noun] The part of a plant that blossoms: roses, daisies, etc.

fly (fl-ah-y) [noun], [verb]
1. A small, winged insect.
2. To travel above the ground, through the air, or to move through the air using wings.

follow (fawl-oh) [verb] To move behind someone or something that you are tracking.

food (f-ood) [noun] Things that people and animals eat for nourishment.

foot (f-oo-t) [noun] 1. The part of your body that you stand and walk on. The end of the leg, below your ankle. 2. A unit of measurement that equals twelve inches.

football (f-oo-t-bawl) [noun] 1. A game played with two teams in which the goal is to get the ball from one end of the field to the other and score a touchdown. 2. The name of the ball used in the football game. 3. Football can mean the sport of soccer in other parts of the world.

football helmet (f-oo-t-bawl hel-mut) [noun] A piece of sports equipment used to protect a person's head while playing football.

for (f-or) [preposition] Used to indicate a purpose.

force (for-s) [noun] The energy with which you can make something move or change its direction.

forest (for-est) [noun] A large, tree-covered area of land.

forget (for-get) [verb] To not remember.

fork (for-k) [noun] 1. A utensil used for picking up food to eat. It has a handle and three or four prongs. 2. A place where a river, road, or tree divides into two parts.

form (for-m) [noun] 1. The way something is or appears to be. 2. The shape of something. 3. An official document to be filled in with information.

forward (for-werd) [adverb] Toward something in front of you.

found (f-ow-nd) [verb] 1. The past tense of *find*. 2. To start something, such as a company or organization. 3. To make something by pouring molten metal into a mold (founding).

four (f-or) [noun] The whole number after three and before five.

fraction (frak-shun) [noun] Part of a whole.

frame (f-ray-m) [noun] A structure that encloses another structure or picture.

free (fr-ee) [adjective], [verb] 1. Something that does not cost anything. 2. To be unrestricted in every way.

fresh (fr-esh) [adjective] Pleasant, new, or clean.

friend (fr-end) [noun] Someone you trust and spend time with.

frog (fr-og) [noun] A small amphibian that lives near water and is known for its long legs and ability to jump.

from (fr-um) [preposition] Starting at a particular time or place.

front (fr-unt) [adjective], [noun] 1. The furthest forward part. 2. The boundary between two air masses.

fruit (fr-oot) [noun] 1. A type of food classification. 2. Something that grows on trees, bushes, or vines, contains seeds, and can be eaten.

full (f-oo-l) [adjective] 1. Containing as much of something as possible. 2. The opposite of empty.

fun (f-un) [adjective] An exciting or enjoyable activity or experience.

funny (f-un-ee) [adjective] Something that makes you laugh or smile.

35

G

gale (g-ay-l) [noun]
A very strong wind.

game (g-ay-m) [noun]
An activity or sport that people play together following specific rules.

garage (g-uh-rah-z) [noun]
A building or covered area for parking motor vehicles.

garbage (gar-bej) [noun]
Material that has been used and is being thrown away.

garden (g-ahr-den) [noun]
A plot of land, usually near a house, where plants and vegetables grow.

gas (g-a-s) [noun] 1. One of the three main states of matter. 2. A fuel used for heat or energy.

gate (g-ay-t) [noun] The part of a fence that can be opened or closed to enter or exit.

gather (g-ath-er) [verb]
1. To collect things and put them in one place. 2. To come together as a group. 3. To pull material into small folds.

gave (g-ay-v) [verb] The past tense of *give*.

general (jen-er-l) [noun], [adjective] 1. A high-ranking commander in the Armed Forces. 2. Nonspecific when referring to something.

gentle (jen-tul) [adjective]
1. Being careful when handling things so as not to hurt or damage them. 2. A soft, light touch.

geography (jee-og-ruf-ee) [noun] 1. The study of the countries and physical surface of the Earth. 2. The physical properties of an area.

germ (j-erm) [noun]
A microscopic organism that can make you sick.

get (g-et) [verb] To receive or obtain something.

ghost (g-oh-s-t) [noun]
The soul of somebody who is no longer living.

giant (jah-y-unt) [noun]
A person or thing of larger-than-average size.

gift (g-ift) [verb], [noun]
1. To give someone something because you like them or for a special occasion. 2. An item you give or is given to you.

giraffe (juh-ra-f) [noun]
An African mammal with a long neck.

girl (g-erl) [noun] A young female person.

give (g-iv) [verb] 1. To let someone have something. 2. To hand something to someone.

glad (gl-ad) [adjective]
Happy or pleased.

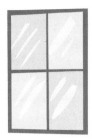

glass (gl-a-s) [noun] 1. A solid, transparent material used for making windows, bottles, glasses, containers, etc. 2. A container made of glass used for drinking.

glasses (gl-a-s-iz) [noun] Glass that has been shaped to assist in vision and placed into frames for wearing.

glove (g-l-uv) [noun] A piece of clothing that covers the hand.

go (g-oh) [verb] To move or travel away from where you are.

goal (g-oh-l) [noun]
1. Something that you intend to achieve in the future.
2. The area usually between two posts, or into a net, of which a ball must go in order to score in a game. 3. When a ball goes into a goal.

goalie (g-oh-l-ee) [noun] Someone on a sports team who stops the other team from scoring goals.

goat (g-oh-t) [noun] A hairy mammal that produces milk that can be turned into cheese.

goggles (g-og-lz) [noun] Specialty glasses for eye protection.

gold (g-oh-ld) [noun]
1. A yellow metal of great value used to make jewelry, coins, awards, and decorations.
2. The color of the metal gold.

goldfish (g-oh-ld-fish) [noun] A small, orange fish often kept as a pet.

golf (g-awl-f) [noun] A sport in which people have to hit a ball into a hole in as few strokes as possible.

golf club (g-awl-f k-luh-b) [noun] The object used to hit a ball in golf.

gone (g-on) [verb], [adjective]
1. The past tense of go.
2. When something no longer exists or is present.

good (g-oo-d) [adjective]
1. Something done well.
2. Something of high quality.

good-bye (g-oo-d-b-ah-y) [interjection] A word used when someone is leaving.

goose (g-oo-s) [noun]
1. A bird similar to a duck, but larger and with a longer neck.
2. A silly person.

gopher (g-oh-fer) [noun] An animal that lives underground.

got (g-ot) [verb] The past tense of get.

gourd (g-oh-r-d) [noun]
A category of fruit that includes fruits such as pumpkins and squash.

govern (gov-ern) [verb]
To control how something happens or is done.

grand (gr-and) [adjective], [noun] 1. Large and impressive. 2. 1,000 American dollars or British pounds.

grandfather (gr-and-fah-th-er) [noun] The father of somebody's parent.

grandmother (gr-and-muh-th-er) [noun] The mother of somebody's parent.

grandparent (gr-and-pair-int) [noun] The parent of somebody's parent.

grape (gr-ay-p) [noun] A small, edible, green, purple, or red fruit that grows on a vine.

grass (gr-a-s) [noun] A plant with thin green leaves that often covers the ground in yards and fields.

grasshopper (gr-a-s-h-aw-per) [noun] An insect that eats grass and is good at hopping.

gray (gr-ay) [adjective] Neutral color; between black and white. The color of dark clouds.

great (gr-ay-t) [adjective] Large, very good, or important.

green (gr-een) [adjective] 1. A secondary color made by mixing blue and yellow. The color of grass and leaves. 2. Not yet mature.

grew (gr-oo) [verb] The past tense of grow.

grill (gr-i-l) [noun]
An outdoor device used to cook food.

ground (gr-ow-nd) [noun], [verb] 1. The surface of the Earth. 2. A particular area of land. 3. To restrict the movement of something. 4. To hit the bottom of the sea with a boat. 5. To connect a piece of electrical equipment to the ground to make it safe.

group (gr-oop) [noun] 1. A gathering of people or things. 2. A number of people connected to each other in a common cause or purpose.

grow (gr-oh) [verb] To become bigger or taller over a period of time.

guard (gaw-rd) [verb], [noun] 1. To protect or contain people or places. 2. Someone whose job is to guard.

guess (g-e-s) [verb] To form an opinion, or answer a question, without enough information to know for certain.

guide (g-ah-y-d) [verb], [noun] 1. To assist the movement of someone or something in a particular direction. 2. To lead or show the way. 3. Someone who guides. 4. A book or digital device that provides instruction.

guitar (g-i-tar) [noun] A musical wooden instrument with six strings that produces sound by strumming the strings with a pick or your fingers.

gumdrops (guh-m-dr-ahp-s) [noun] A colorful and slightly translucent candy typically made from gelatin.

gymnastics (j-im-na-s-t-i-ks) [noun] A sport in which people stretch their bodies and perform stunts.

H

had (h-ad) [verb] The past tense of have.

hail (h-ay-l) [noun] Precipitation in the form of small, hard ice pellets.

hair (h-ay-r) [noun] Thin, thread-like growths on the skin of people and animals.

half (h-af) [noun] One of two parts of something that has been divided equally.

Halloween (h-al-oh-wee-n) [noun] A holiday on October 31 where children dress up in costumes and ask neighbors for candy.

hamburger (ham-ber-ger) [noun] Flat, round beef patties cooked and served on a bun with various toppings.

hammock (ham-uk) [noun] A bed made of a mesh material that hangs in the air by being tied to two poles.

hand (h-and) [noun] The part of the human body at the end of the arm, past the wrist, including the fingers and thumb.

handbag (h-and-b-ag) [noun] A small purse used to hold objects.

handle (h-an-dl) [noun] The part of an object used to hold or control it.

happen (hap-un) [verb] To take place or occur.

happy (hap-ee) [adjective] Feelings of pleasure or well-being.

hard (hah-rd) [adjective]
1. Difficult to do or understand.
2. Solid, stiff, or difficult to bend or break.

harmonica (h-ahr-maw-ni-kuh) [noun] A wind instrument played by blowing air into or out of the holes and moving your lips from side to side to get different notes.

harvest (hah-r-vest) [noun], [verb] 1. The time for gathering crops from the fields.
2. The crops that are gathered.
3. To gather crops.

has (h-a-z) [verb] The third person present tense of have.

hat (h-at) [noun] An article of clothing worn on the head.

have (h-av) [verb] To possess something.

he (hee) [pronoun] Used when referring to a man, boy, or male animal that has been previously mentioned or known.

head (h-ed) [noun] The top of the body above the neck.

hear (h-eer) [verb] To perceive a sound with the ears.

heard (h-er-d) [verb] The past tense of *hear*.

hearing aid (hee-r-ing ay-d) [noun] A device that helps people hear.

heart (hah-rt) [noun]
1. The large, strong muscle in your chest that pumps the blood throughout your body.
2. A basic shape. 3. A symbol representing love.

heat (h-eet) [noun], [verb]
1. A high level of temperature.
2. To make something hot.

heavy (hev-ee) [adjective] Weighing a lot; something that takes great force to lift.

heel (h-eel) [noun]
1. The curved back part of your foot. 2. The curved back part of a shoe or sock. 3. The base of your hand.

height (h-ah-yt) [noun] A measurement of how tall someone or something is or how high it is above the ground.

held (h-el-d) [verb] The past tense of *hold*.

helicopter (hel-ik-op-ter) [noun] A wingless, flying vehicle that uses large, horizontal, rotating blades to fly.

hello (h-el-oh) [interjection] An expression used as a greeting.

helmet (hel-mut) [noun] A protective hat made of hard, strong material often covering the entire head.

help (h-elp) [verb] To make a situation better, easier, or less painful.

hen (h-en) [noun] A full-grown female bird, usually referring to a chicken.

her (h-er) [pronoun] Used when referring to a woman, girl, or female animal that has been previously mentioned or known.

here (h-eer) [adverb] Used when referring to the place that you are currently.

hero (h-eer-oh) [noun] A person of great courage or ability.

high (h-ah-y) [adjective] At a great distance upward.

hill (h-ill) [noun] An elevated area of land smaller than a mountain.

him (h-im) [pronoun] Used when referring to a man, boy, or male animal who has been previously mentioned or known.

hippopotamus (hip-oh-pot-uhm-us) [noun] An African mammal with thick, gray skin that spends much of its time in shallow water.

his (h-iz) [pronoun] Possessive form of the word *he*. Used when talking about something a man, boy, or male animal possesses.

history (his-tor-ee) [noun] Everything that has happened in the past.

hit (h-it) [verb] To strike something with force.

hockey (h-aw-kee) [noun] A sport usually played on ice with a puck in which teams try to score goals by hitting the puck into a net.

hog (h-aw-g) [noun] A large pig

hold (h-oh-ld) [verb] 1. To cause something to remain in place. 2. To grasp something with you hands or arms.

hole (h-oh-l) [noun] An empty space in something solid.

home (h-oh-m) [noun]
1. The place where you live.
2. The place where you feel you belong.

hotel (h-oh-tel) [noun] A building that provides temporary housing, such as on vacation.
hour (ow-r) [noun] A 60-minute unit of time.

honey (h-uh-nee) [noun] Sweet, yellow substance made by bees.
hoof (h-oo-f) [noun] A substance that covers the foot of some animals, such as horses.
hook (h-oo-k) [noun] A curved piece of metal.

hopscotch (h-aw-p-sk-aw-tch) [noun] A game played by skipping across a set of numbers.
horn (h-or-n) [noun] 1. A hard, pointed growth on the head of an animal. 2. An instrument for producing sound.
horse (h-or-s) [noun] A farm animal used to ride or pull farm equipment or carriages. Horses are also used in races as a sport.

house (h-ow-s) [noun] A building where people live together.
how (h-ow) [adverb] Used to ask about the way something is done.

hose (h-oh-z) [noun] A long rubber or plastic tube that is used to put water onto gardens, put out fires, etc.
hot (h-ot) [adjective] A high temperature.

hoop (h-oo-p) [noun] A hole for a ball to go through, typically in basketball.
hope (h-oh-p) [verb] To wish that something you want to happen will happen, or that something you want to be true is.

hot dog (h-ot d-aw-g) [noun] An oblong piece of meat often eaten between a bun.

hug (h-ug) [noun], [verb] 1. An embrace between two people. 2. To embrace someone.
huge (h-yoo-j) [adjective] Something that is very large in size.
human (h-yoo-man) [noun] A person.
hundred (hun-dr-ed) [noun] The whole number after 99 and before 101. The first three-digit number.
hunt (h-unt) [verb] 1. To search for something. 2. To track animals that can be eaten.
hurry (her-ee) [verb] To do something or go somewhere quickly.

43

I

I (ah-y) [pronoun] Used when speaking or writing about yourself.

ice (ah-y-s) [noun] The frozen, solid form of water.

ice cream (ah-y-s kr-eem) [noun] Delicious, sweet frozen food made from milk, cream, sugar, and flavorings.

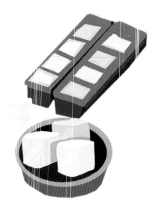

ice cube (ah-y-s k-yoo-b) [noun] A frozen piece of water used to cool drinks.

ice skate (ah-y-s s-kay-t) [noun], [verb] 1. A type of shoe worn to glide across ice. 2. To skate across ice.

iceberg (ah-y-s-berg) [noun] A large, solid mass of ice floating in the sea.

icicle (ah-y-s-ikl) [noun] A funnel-shaped mass of hanging ice formed by dripping and freezing water.

icing (ah-y-s-ing) [noun] A sweet topping used to decorate and flavor cakes or other pastries.

idea (ah-y-dee-uh) [noun] An image in your mind of what something is like or could be like.

identification (ah-y-den-tuh-fi-kay-shun) [noun] A card that has details explaining who you are.

if (if) [conjunction] Used when talking about something that might happen.

iguana (ig-wawn-uh) [noun] A reptile with a spiky back.

ill (il) [adjective] 1. Not feeling well. 2. Being sick.

illustration (il-uh-st-ray-shun) [noun] 1. An example of how to do something. 2. A drawing.

imagine (im-a-jin) [verb] To form an image in your mind of what something is like or should be like.

immediately (im-eed-ee-it-lee) [adverb] Right away.

impossible (im-pos-ibl) [adjective] Something that cannot happen or cannot be done.

in (in) [adjective], [preposition] 1. Into or inside somewhere or something. 2. The opposite of out.

inch (in-ch) [noun] A small, standard unit of measurement.

include (in-kl-ood) [verb] To make someone or something part of a larger group.

indicate (in-di-kayt) [verb] To show what you are referring to.

indoors (in-dor-z) [adverb] Inside a building.

industry (in-dust-ree) [noun] The production of goods or services.

infant (in-funt) [noun] A baby or young child.

injure (in-jer) [verb] To hurt someone or something.

ink (ing-k) [noun] Colored liquid used for writing or drawing.

insect (in-sekt) [noun] A small invertebrate animal with multiple sets of legs.

inside (in-sah-y-d) [preposition], [adverb] 1. The inner side of something. 2. Something that is within something else.

instant (in-stint) [adjective] Happening immediately or right away.

instructor (in-st-ruh-k-ter) [noun] Someone who explains how to do something, such as a teacher.

instrument (in-strim-ent) [noun] 1. A tool used to make music. 2. A tool used to perform delicate work.

interest (in-ter-ist) [noun] The state of wanting to know or learn about something.

interview (in-ter-vy-oo) [verb] To ask someone questions to get to know them better.

introduce (in-tro-doos) [verb] 1. To use for the first time. 2. To bring something or someone to a person's attention for the first time.

invent (in-vent) [verb] To create or design something.

inventor (in-vent-er) [noun] A person who invents things for a living.

invisible (in-viz-ibl) [adjective] Transparent or unable to be seen.

invite (in-vah-yt) [verb] To make a request of someone to go somewhere or do something.

Ireland (ah-y-er-l-and) [noun] An island country in Europe next to England.

iron (ah-y-rn) [noun] 1. A strong, hard, magnetic metal. 2. A tool used to press the wrinkles out of clothing.

is (iz) [verb] To be or exist.

island (ah-y-lind) [noun] A piece of land surrounded by water.

it (it) [pronoun] Used when you are talking about something that has already been mentioned.

itch (it-ch) [noun] A sensation that makes you want to scratch yourself.

J

jacket (jak-it) [noun] A piece of clothing that is worn outside of other clothes to keep you warm and dry. It usually has long sleeves.

jack-in-the-box (j-ak-in-thuh-b-aw-ks) [noun] A toy that you crank up that pops out of its box to the rhythm of a song.

jail (j-ay-l) [noun] A place where people who are accused or have been convicted of a crime are housed.

jam (j-am) [noun] A sweet, jelly-based spread made from fruit and sugar.

janitor (j-an-uh-ter) [noun] Someone who cleans buildings.

January (j-an-yoo-ay-ree) [noun] The first month of the year.

jar (j-ah-r) [noun] A cylindrical container made of glass or pottery.

jaw (j-aw) [noun] The bony structure in your face that forms the mouth and contains your teeth.

jealous (jel-us) [adjective] A feeling that causes you to wish you had the same thing that someone else has.

jeans (j-een-z) [noun] A pair of pants made from denim.

jelly (jel-ee) [noun] A sweet, semi-solid spread made from fruit and sugar.

jellyfish (jel-ee-fish) [noun] A marine animal with a jelly-like, bell-shaped body that can sting.

jester (j-es-ter) [noun] Someone who performed tricks to entertain royalty in the past.

jet (j-et) [noun] An aircraft powered by one or more jet engines.

jewel (joo-el) [noun] A cut and polished precious stone.

jewelry (joo-el-ree) [noun] Any personal ornament, such as rings, necklaces, cuff links, earrings, and bracelets, typically made of precious metals or precious stones.

jig (j-ig) [noun] A dance.

jigsaw (jig-saw) [noun] 1. A picture cut up into many shapes that are meant to be put together. 2. A tool used to cut wood.

job (j-ob) [noun] A form of work in which someone gets paid.

jog (j-og) [verb] To run at a slow pace.

join (j-oy-n) [verb] 1. To link or connect something together. 2. To bring more than one thing together.

joke (j-oh-k) [noun] Something someone says to make people laugh.

jolly (jol-ee) [adjective] Full of high spirits; happy and cheerful.

journal (j-uhr-nuh-l) [noun], [verb] 1. A book of blank pages to write thoughts down in. 2. To write thoughts down in a book.

journey (jer-nee) [noun] A long trip.

joy (j-oy) [noun] A feeling of great pleasure and happiness.

joystick (j-oy-st-ik) [noun] A stick used to control video games.

judge (juj) [noun], [verb] 1. An appointed public official who decides cases in a court of law. 2. To form an opinion about someone or something.

jug (j-ug) [noun] A large container for liquids with a slender neck and handle, often with a stopper or cap.

juggle (j-ug-l) [verb] To continually toss objects into the air and catch them, always keeping one in the air while handling the others.

juggler (j-ug-lr) [noun] A person who juggles.

juice (joos) [noun] A liquid drink made from fruits or vegetables.

jumbo (jum-boh) [adjective] A very large person, animal, or thing.

jump (j-ump) [verb] To push off the ground with your legs and feet and raise yourself into the air.

jump rope (j-ump r-ohp) [noun] A rope with two handles on either end that is jumped over as a form of exercise and sport.

junction (junk-shun) [noun] Where two or more things are joined.

June (jy-oo-n) [noun] The sixth month of the year.

jungle (jung-gl) [noun] An area of land overgrown with dense forest, often in a tropical climate.

junk (jung-k) [noun] Something that is useless or broken.

just (j-uh-st) [adjective], [adverb] 1. Something that is morally right or fair. 2. Exactly like something else.

K

K

kangaroo (k-ayn-guh-r-oo) [noun] An Australian mammal that carries its young in a pouch.

karate (kah-rah-tay) [noun] A form of defensive fighting that originated in Japan.

kayak (k-ah-y-ak) [noun] A lighter form of a canoe that usually only holds one person.

kazoo (k-uh-z-oo) [noun] A musical instrument that makes a buzzing sound when blown into.

keen (k-een) [adjective] Showing eagerness or enthusiasm.

keep (k-eep) [verb] To have or retain possession of something.

kennel (keh-n-uhl) [noun] A crate used to hold pets.

kept (k-ept) [verb] The past tense of *keep*.

ketchup (ke-chup) [noun] A sweet, tangy sauce made of tomatoes.

kettle (ket-uhl) [noun] A metal container with a handle used to boil water.

key (kee) [noun] A small piece of shaped metal that fits into a lock in order to unlock it.

keyboard (kee-b-oh-rd) [noun] A part of a computer used to type.

keychain (kee-ch-ay-n) [noun] A metallic ring that holds keys.

kick (kik) [verb] To forcefully strike with the foot.

kilogram (kil-uh-gram) [noun] A unit of measurement in the metric system. It is equal to about two pounds.

kilt (k-il-t) [noun] A pleated, plaid wool cloth traditionally worn like a skirt by men in the Scottish Highlands.

kind (k-ah-y-nd) [noun], [adjective] 1. A group of people or things that have similar characteristics. 2. Having or showing a friendly or considerate nature.

king (k-ing) [noun] The male ruler of an independent state. They inherit the position by being born into the royal family.

kiss (k-i-s) [verb] To put your lips on someone else as a sign of affection.

kitchen (kich-in) [noun] A room that is used to prepare and cook food.

kite (k-ah-y-t) [noun] A toy with a light frame and thin material stretched over it. It is flown in the wind with a long string attached for the flyer to hold onto and navigate with.

kitten (kit-in) [noun] A baby cat.

knee (nee) [noun] The joint between the thigh and the lower leg that allows your leg to bend.

knew (new) [verb] The past tense of *know*.

knife (n-ah-yf) [noun] A cutting instrument with a blade and a handle.

knight (n-ah-yt) [noun] A mounted soldier in armor.

knit (nit) [verb], [adjective] 1. To make loops of wool or yarn with knitting needles or on a machine. 2. Made of woven or knitted material.

knob (nob) [noun] 1. The part of a door that you use to open it. 2. A lump on the surface of something.

knock (nok) [verb] To strike a surface noisily to attract attention.

knot (not) [noun] A fastener made by tying a piece of string, rope, or something similar.

know (n-oh) [verb] To be aware of something by making an observation or learning about it.

koala (ko-ah-luh) [noun] An Australian mammal that eats eucalyptus leaves and lives in trees.

A B C D E F G H I J K L M N O P Q R S T U V W X Y Z

L

label (lay-bel) [noun] A small piece of paper, fabric, or plastic attached to an object, giving information about it.

ladder (lad-er) [noun] A tool with bars or steps between two poles used to climb up or down from something.

ladle (lay-d-uhl) [noun] A spoon that has a cup-like indention to hold more liquid.

lady (lay-dee) [noun] A polite or formal way to refer to a woman.

ladybug (lay-dee-bug) [noun] A small beetle, typically red or yellow, with black spots.
lake (lay-k) [noun] A large body of water surrounded by land. It is bigger than a pond but smaller than an ocean.

lamb (l-am) [noun] A baby sheep.

lamp (l-amp) [noun] A device that produces light, often powered by electricity or gas.
land (l-and) [noun] The part of the Earth's surface that is not covered by water.
lane (lay-n) [noun] A narrow road, often in a rural area.
language (lang-gwij) [noun] 1. Spoken or written communication. 2. Words and sentences used to communicate from person to person. There are different languages in different parts of the world.

lantern (l-ant-ur-n) [noun] An object that houses a light, typically a candle or bulb, and protects it from wind and rain.
large (lah-rj) [adjective] Bigger than average.
last (l-ast) [adjective] 1. When something comes at the end of something in time or order. 2. The most recent thing to occur before what is happening now.
late (l-ay-t) [adjective] Doing something after the expected time.

laugh (laf) [verb] To express happiness or pleasure through a vocal sound.
launch (lon-ch) [verb] To set something in motion or release it, often referring to a boat or a rocket.
laundry (lon-dree) [noun] Clothing and linens that need to be washed or that have just been washed.
law (l-aw) [noun] The rules that a country or community makes. These rules may be enforced by the police.

lawn (l-on) [noun] A short, grassy area in a yard, garden, or park.

lawnmower (l-on-moh-er) [noun] A device that cuts grass.
lay (l-ay) [verb] To gently place something or yourself down to rest.
lead (l-eed) [verb] 1. To go before someone or with someone to show them the way. 2. To guide something.

leaf (l-eef) [noun] The usually green part of a plant that is attached to the stem.
learn (l-er-n) [verb] To gain knowledge or skill in something by studying, being taught, or through experience.
least (lee-st) [adjective] The smallest amount or degree.
leave (l-eev) [verb] To go away from where you are.
led (l-ed) [verb] The past tense of *lead*.
left (l-eft) [verb], [noun] 1. The past tense of *leave*. 2. The direction opposite of right.
leg (l-eg) [noun] 1. The part of a human or animal body that is used to walk or stand on. 2. The part of a piece of furniture on which it stands.

lemon (lem-in) [noun] A small, yellow fruit known for its sour taste.

lemonade (lem-in-ayd) [noun] A sweet drink made from lemon juice, water, and sugar.
length (lengk-th) [noun] 1. The longest measurement of something from one end to the other. 2. The amount of time something takes.
less (l-es) [adjective] 1. A smaller amount of something. 2. Not as much.
let (l-et) [verb] To allow something.

letter (let-er) [noun] 1. A symbol or character used to form words. There are 26 letters in the English alphabet. 2. Written communication to another person.
level (lev-uhl) [adjective], [noun] 1. Flat or even. 2. An instrument for making sure something is level.

library (lah-y-br-airee) [noun] A place that is full of books and other materials for reading and viewing that can be borrowed.
lie (lah-y) [verb] 1. To say something that is not true on purpose. 2. To recline.
life (lah-y-f) [noun] The time period during which people, plants, or animals eat, drink, grow, and reproduce.

lifeboat (lah-y-f-b-oht) [noun] 1. A boat launched from land to rescue people in distress at sea. 2. A small boat attached to a large one for the purpose of saving passengers if the large boat fails.
lift (l-ift) [verb] To raise an object up.

light (lah-yt) [noun], [adjective] 1. Something that makes things visible. 2. Pale or not deep in color. 3. The opposite of heavy.

light bulb (lah-yt b-uhl-b) [noun] A device that provides light for a room.

lightning (lah-yt-ning) [noun] 1. An electrical discharge between a cloud and the ground. 2. A flash of bright light in the sky.
like (lah-yk) [verb] Taking pleasure in or enjoying someone or something.

line (lah-yn) [noun] A long, narrow mark.

lion (l-ah-y-un) [noun] An African mammal. Male lions have a furry mane while females do not.

lipstick (l-ip-st-ik) [noun] A type of makeup applied to the lips.

liquid (lik-wid) [noun] 1. A state of matter. 2. Something that flows freely and pours easily.
list (l-ist) [noun] A series of names or words written in a meaningful grouping or category.

listen (lis-in) [verb] To pay attention in order to hear something.

litter (li-ter) [noun] Trash that has not been properly thrown away.
little (lit-uhl) [adjective] A small amount of something, or something that is small in size.
live (liv) [verb] To have life or to be alive.

lizard (l-zur-d) [noun] A reptile with a body that rests close to the ground and has short legs and a long tail.

llama (l-aw-muh) [noun] A South American mammal similar to camels but without a hump and much furrier.

lobster (lob-ster) [noun] A large marine animal with stalked eyes and five pairs of limbs. The largest limbs have claws for pinching, crushing, and cutting.

locate (loh-kayt) [verb] To identify or discover a place or location.

lock (l-aw-k) [noun] An object that keeps something closed until unlocked, typically with a key.

locket (l-aw-k-et) [noun] A necklace with a clasped piece that can hold a small object or picture.

log (l-og) [noun] A part of the trunk or limb of a fallen tree.

lone (l-oh-n) [adjective] Being alone.

long (l-ong) [adjective] Having considerable length or lasting a long time.

look (l-oo-k) [verb] To turn your eyes toward something in order to see it.

lost (l-aw-st) [verb], [adjective]
1. To no longer have something.
2. Not been found.

lot (l-ot) [noun] An area of empty land intended for building.

loud (l-ow-d) [adjective] Having great volume or sound.

love (l-uv) [noun], [verb]
1. A warm attachment or deep emotion for someone.
2. To act kindly and selflessly toward someone.

low (l-oh) [adjective] 1. Not far above the ground. 2. Feeling sad.

luggage (lug-ij) [noun] A case for carrying items: suitcases, trunks, or baggage.

lumberjack (lum-ber-j-ak) [noun] A person whose job is to cut down trees and plant seedlings in their place.

lunch (l-un-ch) [noun] A meal usually eaten in the middle of the day.

57

M

macaroni (m-ak-uh-roh-nee) [noun] A type of pasta that is commonly eaten with a cheese sauce.

machine (mush-een) [noun] A tool to help us do work that is made up of one or more mechanisms, such as levers, wheels, axles, and pulleys.

made (m-ay-d) [verb] The past tense of *make*.

magazine (mag-uh-zee-n) [noun] A subscription-service booklet filled with photographs, stories, and educational material.

magic (maj-ik) [noun] The art of performing illusions for entertainment.

magician (muh-jish-un) [noun] Someone who performs magic.

magnet (mag-nit) [noun] A piece of metal or steel that has the ability to attract certain substances, such as iron.

magnetic (mag-net-ik) [adjective] Having the ability to attract.

magnify (mag-nif-ah-y) [verb] Making something look larger than it is.

mail (may-l) [noun], [verb] 1. Letters and packages delivered to a home. 2. To send letters or packages.

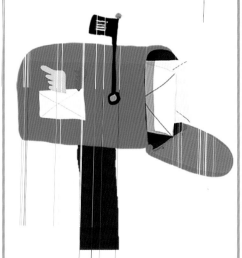

mailbox (may-l-bok-s) [noun] An object in which mail is placed by mail carriers.

main (m-ay-n) [adjective] Something that is decided to be the most important of a group of things.

major (may-jer) [noun], [adjective] 1. A high-ranking military officer. 2. A course of study in college or university. 3. Main, notable.

make (may-k) [verb] 1. To produce something. 2. To shape material or combine things to create something.

mall (m-ahl) [noun] A large building that contains a variety of stores.

mammal (m-am-ul) [noun] A type of animal that typically gives live birth and produces milk.

man (m-an) [noun] An adult male person.

many (m-en-ee) [adjective] 1. More than a few. 2. A large number of something.

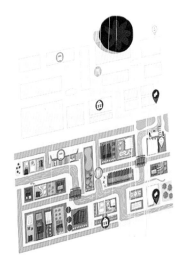

map (m-ap) [noun] A sketch or drawing showing the parts of the Earth's land and water. Maps can show places as small as a neighborhood, or as large as a state, a country, or the entire world.

march (m-ahr-ch) [verb], [noun] 1. To walk in unison with a group. 2. The third month of the year (March).

mark (mah-r-k) [noun] A line, cut, dent, or stain on something.

market (mah-r-k-it) [noun]
A place where people go to
buy and sell things.
marketplace (mah-r-k-it-play-s)
[noun] An open area in a town
where a market is held.
marry (may-r-ee) [verb] To
pledge your love to another
and promise to stay with them
forever.
mask (m-ask) [noun] Something
you can wear to cover all or part
of your face in order to hide it
or to disguise it.
mass (m-a-s) [noun] A large
number or collection of
something.
master (m-a-st-er) [noun]
A person who is very skilled at
something.

match (m-ach) [noun]
1. A person or something that
is equal to or looks the same
as another. 2. A small stick of
wood or paper with flammable
chemicals on the tip used to
light a fire.
material (mat-eer-ee-uhl) [noun]
Things that can be used to
make something else. Fabric,
metal, wood, and plastic are all
materials.
matter (mat-er) [noun]
Something that occupies space.
Everything around us is matter.
may (m-ay) [verb], [noun]
1. To possibly do or say
something. 2. The fifth month
of the year (May).
me (m-ee) [pronoun] Used when
referring to yourself.
meadow (med-oh) [noun] A flat
area of grassy land, often used
for grazing animals.

meal (m-eel) [noun] When food
is served and eaten. There
are three main meals a day:
breakfast, lunch, and dinner.
mean (m-een) [adjective], [verb]
1. Lacking in kindness.
2. To have an idea or intention
in mind.
meant (men-t) [verb] The past
tense of *mean*.
measure (me-zur) [verb] To find
the size, length, or amount of
something.

meat (m-eet) [noun] The flesh
of animals used for food.

meatball (m-eet-bawl) [noun]
A ball made of meat that is
often served with a tomato
sauce and spaghetti.
medicine (med-uh-sin) [noun]
1. Anything used for treating
disease or sickness.
2. The medical profession.
meet (m-eet) [verb] 1. To be
introduced to someone for the
first time. 2. To join up with
someone at an agreed upon
time or place.

melody (mel-uh-dee) [noun]
Musical sounds in sequence
that form an enjoyable tune.

melt (m-elt) [verb] To go from a
solid to a liquid when heated.
men (m-en) [noun] More than
one adult male human.

menu (m-en-yoo) [noun]
A pamphlet or piece of
paper that tells what items a
restaurant serves.
metal (met-uhl) [noun] A solid
substance that is usually hard
and shiny. There are many types
of metal: gold, silver, steel, etc.

meter (meet-er) [noun]
A standard unit of measurement used in the metric system equal to 39.37 inches.

method (meth-uhd) [noun]
A way of doing something.

mice (m-ah-y-s) [noun] More than one mouse.

middle (mid-l) [adjective]
1. To be in between two things.
2. Exactly the same distance from the sides of something.

midnight (mid-nah-yt) [noun]
1. The middle of the night.
2. Twelve o'clock at night.

might (m-ah-yt) [verb], [noun]
1. The past tense of *may*.
2. The power to do something.

mile (m-ah-yl) [noun] A standard unit of measuring distance equal to 5,280 feet.

milk (mil-k) [noun] The liquid that comes from mammals, particularly cows and goats, used to feed their young.

million (mil-ee-uhn) [noun]
A large number that is equal to one thousand times one thousand: 1,000,000.

mind (m-ah-y-nd) [noun]
The part of a human that allows them to think, reason, and feel emotion.

mine (m-ah-y-n) [noun], [pronoun] 1. An underground area where a natural, valuable element is collected: coal mine, diamond mine, etc. 2. A word referring to the ownership of something.

minute (min-it) [noun]
A standard measurement of time equal to 60 seconds.

miss (m-i-s) [verb] 1. To feel sad when not around someone or something. 2. To fail to engage with something.

mittens (m-it-ens) [noun] Pieces of clothing worn on the hands to maintain warmth.

mix (m-iks) [verb] To combine or put together more than one thing to make something different.

mixer (m-iks-er) [noun]
A kitchen appliance used for baking.

modern (mod-ern) [adjective]
Describes something that happens or exists in the present or very recent past.

mold (m-oh-ld) [noun]
A group of fungi that appears on decaying organic items, such as foods.

molecule (mahl-uh-kyool) [noun] A group of atoms stuck together, making it the smallest unit of an element.

moment (moh-ment) [noun]
A very short period of time.

money (mun-ee) [noun] Coins, bills, or bank notes exchanged to purchase something you want or need.

monkey (m-un-kee) [noun]
A type of primate that has a tail.

month (mun-th) [noun] One of the twelve periods of time that a year is divided into (January, February, March, April, May, June, July, August, September, October, November, December).

moon (m-oon) [noun]
The natural satellite of the Earth. The moon can be seen in the sky, mostly at night.

more (m-oh-r) [adjective]
A greater amount of something.

morning (mohr-ning) [noun]
The beginning of the day.

most (m-oh-st) [adjective]
Having the greatest amount or to the greatest degree.

mother (m-uh-ther) [noun]
1. Mom. 2. A female parent.

motion (m-oh-shun) [noun]
The action of moving or being moved.

mount (m-ow-nt) [verb] To climb or to get on top of something.

mountain (m-ownt-in) [noun]
1. A large, natural elevation on the Earth's surface. 2. A very high hill.

mouse (m-ow-s) [noun]
1. A small animal in the rodent family with large ears and a long tail. 2. The part of a computer that you move to select or change things on the screen.

moustache (m-us-ta-sh) [noun] Hair that appears above the lip.
mouth (m-ow-th) [noun] The opening on the face that humans and animals put food into and speak or make sounds out of.
move (m-oo-v) [verb] To pass from one place or position to another.
much (m-uch) [determiner] A large amount of something.
mug (m-ug) [noun] A large cup, usually with a handle made out of ceramics or another heavy material.
multiply (m-ult-ip-lah-y) [verb] 1. To increase the number of something. 2. To perform the process of multiplication.
museum (myoo-zee-uhm) [noun] A building where special or valuable artifacts are stored and put on display.

mushroom (m-uh-sh-roo-m) [noun] A type of fungus that grows in the ground or on trees with a white stalk and a domed cap, some of which are edible.

music (myoo-zik) [noun] Vocal or instrumental sounds that form a beautiful expression of emotion.
must (m-uh-st) [verb] Describing when there is something you should do or are required to do.

mustard (m-uhs-tuh-rd) [noun] A yellow, tangy condiment used to flavor food.
my (m-ah-y) [pronoun] A word you use when you are talking about something that belongs to you.

N

nail (nay-l) [noun] 1. A small metal rod with a flat end used to join two things together when hit with a hammer. 2. The hard, flat surface at the top of each finger and toe (fingernail, toenail).

name (nay-m) [noun] A word or set of words that a person, place, or thing is known by or called.

nametag (nay-m-ta-g) [noun] An object someone attaches to their body so others can know their name.

napkin (n-ap-ki-n) [noun] A cloth made of fabric or paper used to clean up a mess.
narrow (nay-row) [adjective] To be long and thin.
nation (nay-shun) [noun] A large number of people who live in a common area and feel a sense of unity or common purpose.
natural (nach-er-uhl) [adjective] 1. Caused by nature. 2. Not human-made.

nature (nay-cher) [noun] Things that exist without the interference of humans: mountains, trees, rivers, animals, etc.

navy (nay-vee) [noun]
1. A branch of the Armed Forces that works on ships at sea. 2. A dark blue color
near (n-eer) [adjective] A short distance away.

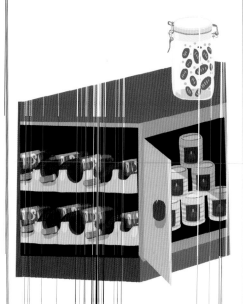

neat (n-eet) [adjective]
An orderly, clean arrangement of things.
necessary (nes-uh-say-ree) [adjective] Describing something that you must do.
neck (n-ek) [noun] 1. The part of a human or animal that connects the head to the rest of the body. 2. The thin part at the top of a bottle or vase.

necktie (n-ek-t-ah-y) [noun]
A piece of fabric that is tied around the neck or the collar of a shirt.

need (n-eed) [verb] Something that is required or necessary.

needle (n-ee-d-uhl) [noun]
A sharp, thin piece of metal used to sew or stick things in place.
neighbor (nay-ber) [noun]
A person living near or next door to you.
nervous (ner-vus) [adjective]
1. A feeling of unease.
2. Anxious that something bad will happen.

nest (n-est) [noun] A bowl-like structure built from mud and twigs by a bird to house its eggs and babies.

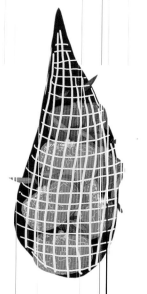

net (n-et) [noun] An open mesh bag made of rope, twine, or thread used to catch or hold something.

never (nev-er) [adjective], [adverb] At no time in the past, present, or future.
new (n-oo) [adjective]
1. Something that was just made or introduced for the first time. 2. The opposite of old.

news (n-ooz) [noun] The report of a recent event or new information.

newspaper (nooz-pay-per) [noun] A published paper written daily or weekly reporting local, national, or world news.
next (nek-st) [adjective] Coming immediately after something.

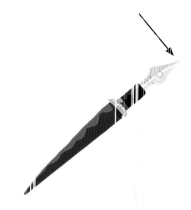

nib (n-ib) [noun] The point of a pen.

night (n-ah-yt) [noun]
The period of darkness between sunset and sunrise.
nine (n-ah-yn) [noun] The whole number after eight and before ten.
no (n-oh) [interjection]
A negative term to show dissent or refusal to do something.
noise (n-oy-z) [noun] A sound.
nonsense (non-sens) [noun]
Words that do not make sense.

noodles (n-oo-dul-z) [noun]
A type of pasta originating in Italy and China.
noon (n-oon) [noun] 1. Twelve o'clock. 2. In the middle of the day.
nor (n-ohr) [conjunction] A word used when two negatives are in one sentence.

north (n-ohr-th) [noun] 1. One of the four cardinal directions. 2. The direction that compass needles always point.

nose (n-oh-z) [noun] The part of the face on humans and most animals that has nostrils and is used to breathe and smell.
nostril (n-ah-s-tuh-rul) [noun]
The hole at the bottom of a nose.

note (n-oh-t) [noun] 1. A short, written statement used to communicate or help remind you of something later.
2. A symbol representing a musical sound.

notebook (n-oh-t-b-oo-k) [noun] 1. A book filled with hanwritten notes. 2. A name for a laptop computer that folds in half.
nothing (nuth-ing) [noun] Not anything.
notice (n-oh-tis) [verb], [noun] 1. To pay attention or look at something. 2. A verbal or written announcement.
noun (n-ow-n) [noun] A part of speech representing a person, place, or thing.

now (n-ow) [adjective]
Something happening at the present time or at this moment.

number (num-ber) [noun]
A symbol representing an amount of something used for counting and calculating.
numeral (noom-er-uhl) [noun]
A symbol representing a number.
nurse (ner-s) [noun] A person trained to take care of sick people, often in a hospital.
nursery (ner-ser-ee) [noun]
1. A room or building used for caring for young children.
2. A building housing plants and small trees.

nut (n-ut) [noun] 1. Dry fruit with a hard outer shell and a soft kernel inside. 2. It can also be the seed from a plant.

nutcracker (n-ut-k-ra-ker) [noun]
A device that cracks nuts.

O

oak (oh-k) [noun] A hardwood tree with acorns and leaves that fall off in the cold months and regrow in the spring.

oar (oh-r) [noun] A pole with a flat blade used to row or steer a boat.

oasis (oh-ay-sis) [noun] A small, green, fertile area in the desert that has water.

obey (oh-bay) [verb] To do what someone has told you to do.

object (ob-jekt) [noun], [verb] 1. Anything that can be seen and touched. 2. To oppose.

observe (ob-zerv) [verb] To see or to watch something.

occupation (ok-yoo-pay-shun) [noun] 1. A person's work or business. 2. How a person earns a living.

occur (uh-ker) [verb] To happen or to take place.

ocean (oh-shun) [noun] The large body of salt water that covers almost three-quarters of the Earth's surface.

octagon (ok-tuh-gah-n) [noun] A shape with eight sides and eight vertices.

octopus (ok-tu-p-oo-s) [noun] A marine animal with a soft, round body and eight legs covered in suction cups.

odd (aw-d) [adjective] To be different, not ordinary, unusual.

of (uv) [preposition] A word used when expressing the relationship between a part and a whole.

off (aw-f) [preposition], [adverb] 1. No longer attached to something. 2. Away from a place or position.

offer (aw-fer) [verb] Presenting something for acceptance or rejection.

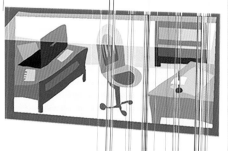

office (aw-fis) [noun] A room or building where work is done.

officer (aw-fis-er) [noun] 1. A high-ranking person in the Armed Forces. 2. A member of the police department.

often (awf-tuhn) [adverb] Something happening many times or frequently.

oh (oh) [interjection] An expression of surprise or pain.

oil (oy-l) [noun] A thick liquid that has many uses depending on what it is made of. Petroleum oil is used for fuel. Vegetable, coconut, and peanut oils are used for cooking.

ointment (oynt-muhnt) [noun] A soft, thick balm that is rubbed on the skin for medical or cosmetic reasons.

okra (oh-k-ruh) [noun] A type of vegetable commonly grown in tropical and warm climates.

old (oh-ld) [adjective] Having lived or existed for a long time.

olive (ah-l-iv) [noun] A small, dark green or black fruit grown from an olive tree.

on (ah-n) [preposition], [adverb] 1. Being connected to something or supported by something. 2. Functioning.

once (wun-s) [adverb] Something that happened at one time in the past.

one (wun) [noun] 1. The lowest whole number. 2. The whole number before two. 3. A single thing.

onion (un-ee-un) [noun] A type of vegetable with a skin around it that can cause people to cry when cut.

only (ohn-lee) [adverb] Being by yourself or without others.

open (oh-pin) [adjective] 1. Not closed. 2. Having access to something.

opera (op-ruh) [noun] 1. A type of music. 2. A dramatic play in which all of the parts are sung.

operate (op-uh-rayt) [verb] To have control of a machine.

opossum (p-aw-sum) [noun] A North American mammal that often plays dead to avoid being attacked by predators or humans.

opposite (op-uh-sit) [adjective] To have or take position on the farthest side of something or to take a contrary position.

or (or) [conjunction] A word used to connect words when you are giving choices or alternatives.

orange (or-anj) [noun] 1. A color made by mixing red and yellow. 2. An orange fruit that grows from trees and is often juiced or eaten as a snack.

orange juice (or-anj joos) [noun] Juice made from squeezing oranges.

orca (or-kuh) [noun] A type of whale known for its black-and-white appearance.

orchard (or-cherd) [noun] An area of land used for growing fruit trees.

orchestra (ork-uh-struh) [noun] A group of performers playing musical instruments.

order (or-der) [verb], [noun] 1. To command someone to do something. 2. A command given by an authority figure.

organ (or-gin) [noun] 1. A large musical instrument with many long pipes, played by a keyboard. 2. A group of tissues in the body that perform important functions: heart, liver, kidney, etc.

original (uh-rij-uh-nl) [adjective] 1. The first of something or the beginning of something. 2. Something new or novel.

orb (or-b) [noun] A spherical object.

ornament (orn-uh-ment) [noun] A decoration used to make something more pleasing to the eye.

other (uh-ther) [adjective]
A word used when talking about a person or thing that is different from what you are talking about.

our (ow-r) [pronoun] A word used when you are talking about more than one person and ownership of something.

out (ow-t) [adjective]
1. Opposite of *in*. 2. Away or outside of an enclosed structure.

oval (oh-vuhl) [noun], [adjective] Having the form, shape, or outline of an egg.

oven (uh-vin) [noun]
An appliance used for cooking food.

over (oh-ver) [preposition]
Something that is above.

overalls (oh-ver-awl-z) [noun]
A style of pants that also covers part of the chest.

owl (ow-l) [noun] A large nocturnal bird of prey with a hooked beak, sharp talons, and big, round eyes.

own (oh-n) [verb] A word used when you are talking about something that belongs to you.

ox (aw-ks) [noun] A large, male animal that is part of the bovine family (bull), often used for heavy labor on farms.

oxygen (ok-si-juhn) [noun]
A gas with no color or odor that animals and humans need to live.

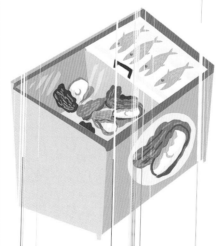

oyster (oy-s-ter) [noun]
A creature with a hard shell that typically attaches to rocks in shallow water on coastlines

P

pack (pak) [noun], [verb]
1. A group of things wrapped or tied together, especially something carried on your back. 2. A group of people, animals, or things. 3. To put things you need in a bag.

paddle (pad-uhl) [noun] A short, flat bladed oar used for rowing or steering a canoe or small boat.

page (pay-j) [noun] One side of a sheet of paper in a book, magazine, or newspaper.

pain (pay-n) [noun]
When something hurts, usually because you have been injured or you are sick.

paint (pay-nt) [noun] A colored liquid that is spread on a surface, such as walls or canvas, to create a decorative or artistic look.

paintbrush (pay-nt-br-uh-sh) [noun] A tool with fine bristles on the end used to paint.

painter (pay-nt-er) [noun]
Someone who creates art with paint.

pair (pay-r) [noun] A set of two things that go together and are considered a unit.

pajamas (puh-jaw-muh-z) [noun] A type of clothing worn when sleeping.

palm (p-awl-m) [noun] The inner part of your hand between your wrist and your fingers.

palm tree (p-awl-m tr-ee) [noun] A branchless tree with distinctive palm leaves that grows in hot, tropical climates.

pancake (pan-kay-k) [noun] A flat, thin cake fried on both sides in a pan or griddle, usually eaten with maple syrup.

panda (p-an-duh) [noun] A black-and-white bear from China.

paper (pay-per) [noun] A thin material usually made from wood pulp used for drawing or writing on or to wrap things.

parachute (pair-uh-shoot) [noun] A harness with a large, folded piece of canvas attached and lines that billow out when released. It is used to slow down the descent of a person or object that is falling from a great height, often from an airplane.

paragraph (pair-uh-graf) [noun] A section of writing that has three to five sentences containing its own idea. Each new paragraph usually begins with an indentation.

parcel (pahr-suhl) [noun] Something wrapped up in paper or packaging.

parent (pair-int) [noun] Someone who is raising a child or children.

park (paw-rk) [noun] An area of land, usually having grass and trees, playgrounds, picnic areas, and walking paths that are used for people to relax and play.

part (paw-rt) [noun] A portion or section of something.

particular (paw-rt-ik-yoo-lur) [adjective] Something special or worth mentioning about one thing out of several things.

party (paw-rt-ee) [noun] 1. A group of people who have gathered at a specific place, usually by invitation, to share conversation, refreshments, and entertainment. 2. A group of people with a common purpose.

pass (p-a-s) [verb] 1. To move past something or to go by something. 2. To let something go without showing interest.

passenger (pas-uhn-jer) [noun] A person traveling in a car, train, plane, boat, or other form of transportation, especially someone who is not the driver of the vehicle.

passport (pas-poh-rt) [noun] An official document that allows someone to travel outside of their home country and is used as identification.

past (p-a-st) [adjective] Something that happened before the present time.

pastry (pay-st-ree) [noun] Sweet, baked food made of dough: muffins, pies, tarts, doughnuts, etc.

patch (p-at-ch) [noun] A piece of fabric used to cover a tear.

path (p-a-th) [noun] A narrow walkway usually through a garden, a park, or a wooded area.

pattern (pat-ern) [noun] A decorative design on something.

paw (p-aw) [noun] The foot of an animal with claws.

pay (p-ay) [verb] To give someone money in exchange for something.

peace (p-ee-s) [noun] A state of harmony between people and groups. Not being at war.

peanut (pee-nut) [noun] The seed of a South American plant that is eaten as a snack and also used for making peanut butter and peanut oil.

pear (pay-er) [noun] A sweet and juicy green fruit.

pearl (p-erl) [noun] A smooth, round bead formed inside of a mollusk shell. It is considered rare and precious and can range in color from black to gray, white, or blush.

pebble (peb-uhl) [noun] A small, round stone worn smooth by water.

pedal (ped-uhl) [noun] A foot-powered lever used to control mechanisms or machines such as cars.

pen (p-en) [noun] 1. An instrument for writing or drawing with ink. 2. A small, fenced area used to contain farm animals: pig pen, sheep pen, etc.

pencil (pen-suhl) [noun] A long, thin tube of wood with a center and tip made of lead or graphite used to draw or write.

penguin (peng-gwin) [noun] A large bird that lives in the Southern Hemisphere and has webbed feet and small, flipper-like wings but cannot fly.

people (pee-puhl) [noun] More than one person.

perfect (per-fikt) [adjective] 1. Something without any flaws or mistakes. 2. Something that is exactly what is wanted or needed.

perform (per-fohr-m) [verb] 1. To act in a play, on stage, or in movies or television. 2. To put on a show for someone. 3. To carry out a task or to do something.

perfume (per-fyoom) [noun] A fluid containing fragrant oils often from flowers, or any agreeable attractive smell.

perhaps (per-hap-s) [adverb] 1. The possibility that something might happen. 2. Maybe.

period (peer-ee-uhd) [noun] 1. A length or portion of time usually a time that is significant for some reason. 2. A punctuation mark used to end statements.

person (per-sun) [noun] Any human being.

pet (p-et) [noun] Any animal that is kept as a companion, loved, and cared for.

phone (fohn) [noun] A device for talking with someone at a distance. Short for telephone.
photo (foh-toh) [noun] A picture made using a camera. Short for photograph.
photographer (foh-tog-ruh-fer) [noun] 1. A person who takes pictures professionally. 2. Someone who has been trained in photography.
phrase (fr-ayz) [noun] A small group of words used together to form an idea or a sentence.
pick (pik) [verb] To choose something from a group.

pickle (pi-k-uhl) [noun] A sour, salty fruit made by brining a cucumber in salt water.
picnic (pik-nik) [noun], [verb] 1. An outing or event where you have a meal or take food outside to eat. 2. To eat outside.

picture (pik-cher) [noun], [verb] 1. A painting or drawing of something. 2. A photograph or any other image of something. 3. To have an idea or image in your mind.

pie (p-ah-y) [noun] A baked pastry dish filled with fruit, vegetables, or meat.
piece (pee-s) [noun] A portion of something made by cutting or tearing it.

pig (p-ig) [noun] A farm animal known for its curly tail, hooves, and flat snout.

pigeon (p-ij-un) [noun] A bird that is often seen in cities.
pillow (pil-oh) [noun] A cloth bag filled with soft materials used to support the head while sleeping.
pilot (p-ah-y-lit) [noun] A person who is in charge of flying an aircraft.

pin (p-in) [noun] A wooden or metallic object used to fasten other objects together.
pitch (p-ich) [verb], [noun] 1. To throw a ball for a batter to try to hit. 2. The degree of highness or lowness or tone of a sound.

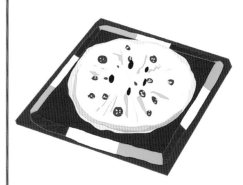

pizza (pee-ts-uh) [noun] A food made of dough, sauce, cheese, and toppings.
place (pl-ay-s) [noun] A specific position.
plain (pl-ayn) [adjective] Simple or ordinary in nature.
plan (pl-an) [noun] A detailed way of accomplishing something.
plane (pl-ay-n) [noun] 1. A flat surface. 2. An aircraft.
planet (plan-it) [noun] A celestial body that orbits around the Sun, such as the Earth or Mars.

plant (pl-ant) [noun] A living organism, such as trees, grass, or flowers.

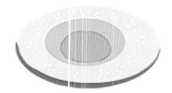

plate (play-t) [noun] A flat object used to serve food.

play (pl-ay) [verb] To take part in an activity for enjoyment rather than for a practical reason.

playground (pl-ay-gr-ow-nd) [noun] A place provided for children to play on.

please (pl-eez) [adverb] A phrase used for polite requests.

plural (pler-uhl) [adjective] More than one.

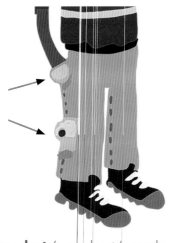

pocket (paw-k-ut/paw-k-et) [noun] Part of clothing used to hold objects.

poem (poh-uhm) [noun] A piece of writing that is usually rhythmic or metaphorical.

point (poy-nt) [verb] To direct attention to something.

police (puh-lees) [noun] A government agent responsible for preventing crime and helping people.

poor (p-oor) [adjective] 1. Not having enough money to live comfortably. 2. Not of good quality.

popcorn (pop-cohrn) [noun] A type of snack food made from corn kernels that burst open when heated.

populate (pop-yuh-layt) [verb] To fill a place.

port (poh-rt) [noun] A town or place with a spot for shipping boats to dock.

pose (poh-z) [noun] A way of sitting or standing, usually for a photograph or painting.

position (poh-zish-un) [noun] A place where something or someone is.

possible (pos-uh-buhl) [adjective] Able to be done.

post (poh-st) [noun], [verb] 1. A long piece of wood or metal. 2. To display in a public place.

postman (poh-st-man) [noun] The person who carries and delivers the mail.

pot (p-ah-t) [noun] 1. A device used in cooking that can hold liquids and sauces. 2. An object that can hold other objects, such as flowers.

potato (puh-tay-toh/poh-tay-toh) [noun] A starchy, root vegetable that is grown underground.

pound (pow-nd) [noun] A unit of measurement when referring to weight.

power (p-ow-er) [noun] The ability to have control over someone or something.

practice (prak-tis) [verb] To perform an activity or exercise repeatedly in order to perfect the action.

prepare (pree-pair) [verb] To make something ready for use.

present (prez-int) [noun]
1. A gift. 2. The current period of time.
press (pr-es) [verb], [noun]
1. To apply pressure.
2. An object used to apply pressure to something: garlic press, printing press, flower press, etc.
pretty (prit-ee) [adjective]
To be attractive.

price (p-rah-y-s) [noun]
How much something costs.
prince (pr-ins) [noun] The son of a king or queen.

princess (prin-ses) [noun]
The daughter of a king or queen.
print (pr-int) [verb], [noun]
1. To produce things such as books or newspapers. 2. The words appearing in printed media.
prize (pr-ah-yz) [noun]
Something given as a reward.
probable (prob-ib-uhl) [adjective] More than possible.
problem (prob-luhm) [noun]
A situation that is difficult to overcome.
process (pros-es) [noun]
A series of actions taken in order to achieve a goal.

produce (proh-doos) [noun]
Something that has been grown, such as fresh fruits and vegetables.
product (prod-ukt) [noun]
An object that is made for sale.
proper (prop-er) [adjective]
The correct and polite way of doing or saying something.
property (prop-er-tee) [noun]
An object or objects belonging to someone.
protect (proh-tekt) [verb]
The action of keeping something or someone safe from harm.
prove (proov) [verb]
To show the existence or fact of something through evidence.
provide (proh-vah-yd) [verb]
To make something available to use.
puddle (pud-uhl) [noun] A small gathering of liquid.
pull (p-oo-l) [verb] To apply force in order to move or try to move something toward yourself.

pumpkin (p-uh-mp-ki-n) [noun]
An orange gourd often used to decorate in fall and for Halloween.

puppy (p-up-ee) [noun]
A young dog.
purple (per-puhl) [noun]
The color made when mixing primary colors red and blue together.
purse (p-ur-s) [noun]
An accessory used to carry objects.

push (p-oo-sh) [verb]
To apply force in order to move or try to move something away from yourself.
put (p-oo-t) [verb] To move or place something in a specific position.
puzzle (puz-uhl) [noun]
An object or problem made to test determination or intelligence.

pyramid (pee-ruh-mid) [noun]
A three-dimensional object consisting of one square face and four triangular faces.

Q

quack (kw-ak) [noun] The sound made by a duck.

quail (kw-ay-l) [noun] A type of bird with a short tail.

quarrel (kwor-uhl) [noun], [verb] 1. An angry disagreement, usually between friends. 2. To disagree with someone loudly.

quart (kw-ohrt) [noun] A unit of liquid measurement equal to two pints or one quarter of a gallon.

quarter (kw-ohrt-er) [noun] 1. A US coin worth twenty five cents. 2. One of four equal parts.

queasy (kw-ee-zee) [adjective] To feel nauseated.

queen (kw-een) [noun] A female who rules over a kingdom.

question (kw-es-chun) [noun], [verb] 1. A sentence posed in a way to get information. 2. To ask questions.

question mark (kw-es-chun m-ahr-k) [noun] A form of punctuation that denotes a question.

quick (kw-ik) [adjective] At a fast speed.

quicksand (kw-ik-s-and) [noun] A form of dirt that pulls objects and animals down into the ground.

quiet (kw-ah-y-it) [adjective] A soft or nonexistent noise.

quill (kw-il) [noun] A feather that is dipped in ink and used to write.

quilt (kw-ilt) [noun] A covering, usually handmade, consisting of patches of fabric stitched together.

quite (kw-ah-yt) [adverb] A word used to describe something of the highest degree; used in place of words, such as *absolutely*.

quiz (kw-iz) [noun] A compilation of questions used to test knowledge.

quotient (kw-oh-sh-uhnt) [noun] The result of division.

R

rabbit (rab-it) [noun] A furry, long-eared mammal that eats plants and burrows in the ground.

raccoon (ra-koo-n) [noun]
A mammal with stripes and a distinct eye mask that often digs through trash for food.

race (ray-s) [noun], [verb]
1. A competition used to determine who or what is the fastest. 2. To compete to see who is the fastest.

racket (ra-ket) [noun] An object used to hit the ball in tennis and other sports.

radar (ray-dawr) [noun]
A device used to emit radio waves to detect and locate objects, such as aircraft or surfaces of planets.

radio (ray-dee-oh) [noun]
A system used to transmit and receive radio frequencies.

radish (rad-ish) [noun] A type of red root vegetable.

raft (ra-ft) [noun] A floating platform used for transportation or relaxation in the water.

rail (ray-l) [noun] Part of a fence or object used as a barrier.

rain (ray-n) [noun]
1. A liquid form of precipitation.
2. Water that falls from clouds in drops.

rainbow (rayn-bow) [noun]
A display of colors in the form of an arch, caused by light from the sun being refracted, usually after the rain.

raincoat (rayn-k-oh-t) [noun]
A type of outerwear worn to protect people from the rain.

raise (ray-z) [verb], [noun]
1. To lift to a higher level.
2. An increase in level of pay.

rake (ray-k) [noun] A tool, resembling a broom, used to gather leaves.

ran (r-an) [verb] The past tense of *run*.

range (ray-nj) [noun] 1. A set of mountains that are next to each other. 2. An area of variation between specified limits.

rather (rath-er) [adverb]
A word used to show preference.

ravioli (rav-ee-oh-lee) [noun] A type of pasta that is filled before being cooked.

reach (ree-ch) [verb] The action of extending an arm in order to touch or grab something.

read (r-eed) [verb] To see and comprehend written words or symbols.

ready (red-ee) [adjective] Prepared mentally or physically for something.

real (r-eel) [adjective] Describes something that is in existence.

reason (ree-zun) [noun] An explanation or cause for an act or event.

receive (ree-seev) [verb] To accept something.

recipe (res-ip-ee) [noun] A list of ingredients and step-by-step guide to preparing something.

record (rek-ohrd) [noun], [verb] 1. A documented piece of evidence about the past. 2. To take note of for later reference.

red (r-ed) [noun] One of the three primary colors.

reed (r-eed) [noun] A piece of tall, coarse grass, similar to bamboo.

referee (ref-er-ee) [noun] The official person who watches and pays attention to a game to make sure players follow the rules.

refrigerator (rif-rij-uh-ray-ter) [noun] An appliance that is used to keep perishables cold.

region (re-jun) [noun] A geographical area distinguished by similar features.

reindeer (rayn-d-ee-r) [noun] A type of animal that lives in high northern regions in very cold climates.

remember (ri-mem-ber) [verb] To recall a certain time or incident from the past.

remote control (ruh-moh-t k-uhn-tr-oh-l) [noun] A device used to control a television or other electronic devices.

repair (ri-payr) [verb] To fix something that is broken.

repeat (ri-peet) [verb] To say or act out something that has already been said or done.

reply (ri-pl-ah-y) [verb] To respond.

report (rip-ohrt) [verb], [noun] 1. To give an account of something that you have witnessed. 2. An account of something.

reporter (rip-ohrt-er) [noun] A person who reports news.

represent (rep-res-ent) [verb] To be appointed to act or speak for someone or something in an official capacity.

reptile (rep-t-ah-yl) [noun] A cold-blooded animal including snakes, lizards, turtles, crocodiles, and tortoises.

require (ree-kw-ah-yr) [verb] To need or depend on.

rescue (res-kyoo) [verb] To save someone or something from danger.

rest (r-est) [verb] To refrain from work or movement in order to recover strength and energy.

restaurant (rest-er-ahnt) [noun] A place where people go and pay to eat a meal.

result (ree-zult) [noun] An outcome.

reward (ree-waw-rd) [noun] Something given for the purpose of recognizing effort.

rhyme (rah-ym) [noun] A word or phrase that sounds the same at the end as another word.

rice (rah-ys) [noun] A type of food that comes from a swamp grass, especially from Asia.

rich (r-ich) [adjective] Having a large amount of money or possessions.

ride (rah-yd) [verb] The act of sitting on and controlling the movement of an object or animal.

right (r-ah-yt) [noun], [adjective]
1. A direction opposite of left.
2. The correct way of doing or saying something.

ring (r-ing) [noun] A small band in the shape of a circle, usually worn on the finger.

rink (r-ing-k) [noun] A place where people skate, either on roller skates or ice skates.

rise (r-ah-yz) [verb] To gently move to a higher position.

river (riv-er) [noun] A body of water occurring in nature flowing into the sea, a lake, or a stream.

road (r-oh-d) [noun] A path leading from one place to another, usually used for cars to drive on.

robin (rob-in) [noun] A small songbird, often with a red breast.

robot (r-oh-bah-t) [noun] A machine that acts like a human.

rock (r-ok) [noun] A solid piece of mineral material.

rocket (rok-it) [noun] A cylindrical object that can be launched to a great height.

rocking horse (r-ok-ing h-or-s) [noun] A toy horse sat on by children that moves back and forth to mimic riding.

roll (r-ohl) [verb] To move by turning over on an axis in repetition.

roof (r-oof) [noun] The upper covering of a house or building.

room (r-oom) [noun] A sectioned off space in a large area.

rooster (r-oo-s-ter) [noun] A male chicken.

root (r-oot) [noun] The base that provides stability and nourishment to a plant.

rope (r-ohp) [noun] A strong, thick cord.

rose (r-ohz) [noun], [verb]
1. A type of shrub that bears a specific type of flower.
2. The past tense of *rise*.

round (r-ow-nd) [adjective] Shaped like a circle.

row (r-oh) [noun], [verb]
1. A collection of people or things in a line. 2. To propel a boat with an oar.

rub (r-ub) [verb] The movement of a hand or cloth on the surface of something.

rug (r-ug) [noun] A floor covering, usually not covering the entire space of a room.

rule (r-ool) [noun] A specific instruction given to maintain order in a group or process.

run (r-un) [verb] To move at a pace faster than walking.

rung (r-ung) [noun] A horizontal support.

s

sack (s-ak) [noun] A bag.

sad (s-ad) [adjective] An emotion of sorrow.

saddle (sad-l) [noun] A leather seat that is fastened on the back of an animal for riding.

safe (s-ayf) [adjective] Protected from danger.

said (sed) [verb] 1. The past tense of *say*. 2. Something already mentioned.

sail (s-ayl) [verb], [noun] 1. To travel in a boat that uses wind in its sails to move. 2. Piece of fabric hung on a boat to harness wind and propel it.

sailboat (s-ayl-boht) [noun] A boat propelled by sails.

salt (s-awlt) [noun] A mineral found in seawater, typically used for taste or preservation of food.

same (s-aym) [adjective] Not different.

sand (s-and) [noun] A substance comprised of eroded rocks and minerals, usually found on beaches.

sandwich (s-and-w-ich) [noun] A food dish that consists of two pieces of bread with fillings in between.

sat (s-at) [verb] The past tense of *sit*.

save (s-ayv) [verb] To rescue.

saw (s-aw) [noun], [verb] 1. A tool used by hand for cutting. 2. The past tense of *see*.

say (s-ay) [verb] To speak.

scale (sk-ayl) [noun] 1. An instrument for weighing objects. 2. The protective skin on fish.

scarecrow (sk-ay-r-k-rch) [noun] An object constructed like a person that is used to scare crows away from crops on a farm.

scarf (sk-ahr-f) [noun] A piece of clothing worn around the neck to keep warm.

school (sk-ool) [noun] An institution where people gather to be taught new information.

science (s-ah-y-uhn-s) [noun] The systematic study of the natural world.

scissors (siz-erz) [noun] A handheld instrument often used for cutting paper, fabric, or hair.

score (sk-ohr) [noun], [verb] 1. The number of points achieved in a game. 2. To earn a point.

sea (s-ee) [noun] A large body of salt water that covers most of the Earth's surface.

search (ser-ch) [verb] To look for someone or something.

season (see-zuhn) [noun] One of the four times of the year marked by changes in weather: spring, winter, summer, or fall.

seat (s-eet) [noun] An object used to sit on.

second (sek-uhnd) [noun] 1. A measurement of time shorter than a minute. 2. Coming after the first.

section (sek-shun) [noun] A specific part of something.

see (see) [verb] To detect something using your eyes.

seed (s-eed) [noun] A part of a plant containing the embryo needed to grow another plant.

seem (s-eem) [verb] To give or appear to have a particular quality.

segment (seg-ment) [noun] A part or section.

select (sel-ekt) [verb] To choose something.

self (s-elf) [noun] A word used when referring to your own body or personality.

sell (s-el) [verb] To exchange something for money.
send (s-end) [verb] To arrange for the delivery of.
sense (s-en-s) [noun], [verb] 1. A way that the body perceives either sight, smell, sound, taste, or touch. 2. To feel like something may happen or be happening.
sent (s-ent) [verb] The past tense of *send*.
sentence (s-ent-en-s) [noun] Words structured as a complete thought to convey information.
separate (sep-er-ayt) [verb] To move objects or parts of an object away from each other.
serve (s-erv) [verb] To perform duties for another person or organization.
set (s-et) [verb] To place something in a certain position.
settle (set-l) [verb] To come to an agreement about an argument or problem.

7

seven (sev-uhn) [noun] The number after six and before eight.
several (sev-er-uhl) [adjective] More than two, but not a lot.
shall (sh-al) [verb] A word used to express a strong intention.
shape (sh-ayp) [noun] The form of someone or something.
share (sh-ayr) [verb] To give or lend a portion of something with others.
sharp (sh-ahrp) [adjective] Describes an object that could cut or pierce something.
she (sh-ee) [pronoun] Used when referring to a woman, girl, or female animal that has been previously mentioned or known.

sheep (sh-eep) [noun] A mammal from the cattle family with a thick, wool coat.
sheet (sh-eet) [noun] A large piece of cotton or fabric normally placed on a bed to cover the mattress.
shell (sh-el) [noun] The hard, protective outer case of an underwater creature.
shine (sh-ah-yn) [verb] To give off a bright light.
ship (sh-ip) [noun] A water vessel larger than a boat.
shoe (sh-oo) [noun] Something worn to cover and protect feet, usually made from leather, rubber, or other materials.
shop (sh-op) [verb] To browse or buy something from a store.
shore (sh-ohr) [noun] The land along the edges of a body of water.
short (sh-ohrt) [adjective] A measurement of a small distance or height.
should (sh-oo-d) [verb] Used to convey obligation.
shoulder (sh-ohl-der) [noun] A joint of the body where the arm attaches to the torso.
shout (sh-owt) [verb] To let out a loud call or cry.
show (sh-oh) [verb] To cause something to be visible.
side (s-ah-yd) [noun] A position on either the left or right of an object or idea.
sight (s-ah-yt) [noun] The ability to see.
sign (s-ah-yn) [noun], [verb] 1. The presence or occurrence of someone or something that indicates the presence or occurrence of something else. 2. A posted board containing information. 3. To communicate with your hands.

silent (s-ah-y-luhnt) [adjective] The absence of sound.
silver (sil-ver) [noun] A precious metal that is shiny and grayish-white in color.
similar (sim-uhl-er) [adjective] Possessing a like quality to something or someone else without being identical.
simple (sim-pl) [adjective] Something that is easily understood.
since (sin-s) [preposition] 1. The period between a specific time in the past and the present. 2. As a result.

sing (s-ing) [verb] To use your voice to make musical sounds.
single (sing-gl) [adjective] One and not multiple.
sink (s-ink) [noun] A basin, usually found in bathrooms or kitchens, including a drain and water supply.
sister (sis-ter) [noun] A woman with whom you share parents.
sit (s-it) [verb] To be in a position in which a person or animal's weight is supported by their buttocks.
six (s-ix) [noun] The number after five and before seven.
size (s-ah-yz) [noun] How big or small something is.
skein (sk-ah-y-n) [noun] A quantity of yarn or thread.
ski (sk-ee) [noun], [verb] 1. A pair of long objects, made from flexible material, used in the sport of skiing. 2. To move your body while wearing skis.

A
B
C
D
E
F
G
H
I
J
K
L
M
N
O
P
Q
R
S
T
U
V
W
X
Y
Z

skill (sk-il) [noun] The ability to carry out an action in a high degree.

skin (sk-in) [noun] The layer of tissue that forms the outer covering of a person.

skunk (sk-un-k) [noun] A black-and-white striped animal that produces a bad smell when threatened.

sky (sk-ah-y) [noun] The area of the atmosphere as seen from Earth.

sled (sl-ed) [noun] A device used to slide down hills, especially over snow. Can be used for fun or for transporting goods.

sleep (sl-eep) [verb] To rest.

slip (sl-ip) [verb] To unintentionally fall a short distance.

slow (sl-oh) [adjective] A low speed.

small (sm-all) [adjective] A size that is less than average.

smell (sm-ehl) [verb], [noun] 1. To detect the odor of something. 2. An odor.

smile (sm-ah-yl) [noun], [verb] 1. The form that a person's mouth often takes when pleased or happy. 2. The movement of your mouth to show happiness.

smoke (sm-oh-k) [noun] Dark-gray particle produced through burning that rises.

snack (sn-ak) [noun] A small amount of food eaten, but not as a meal.

snail (sn-ayl) [noun] An animal with a single spiral shell that their whole body can retract into.

snake (sn-ayk) [noun] A reptile that is long and has no limbs.

sneeze (sn-eez) [verb], [noun] 1. The involuntary action of the expulsion of air from a person or animal's nose. 2. The expulsion of air through a nose.

snow (sn-oh) [noun] A type of precipitation that is frozen.

so (s-oh) [adverb] To an extent.

soda (so-duh) [noun] A carbonated beverage.

sofa (s-oh-fuh) [noun] A long seat that is stuffed and covered with soft materials and is made for two or more people.

soft (s-aw-ft) [adjective] Describes something that is smooth, often fluffy, and easy to compress.

soil (s-oyl) [noun] A layer of earth in which plant life can grow.

soldier (s-ohl-jer) [noun] A person who serves in a governmental position, specifically in the Armed Forces.

solution (sohl-oo-shun) [noun] 1. The answer to a problem. 2. A mixture of liquids.

solve (s-awl-v) [verb] To find a solution.

some (sum) [adjective] A portion of something.

son (s-uhn) [noun] Someone's male child.

song (s-ahn-g) [noun] A set of words, sometimes in the form of a poem, set to music.

soon (s-oon) [adverb] After a short period of time.

sound (s-ownd) [noun] Vibrations that travel and can be heard when they reach a person's ear.

soup (soo-p) [noun] A food dish made from cooking down a liquid and adding seasonings.

south (s-owth) [noun] 1. One of the four cardinal directions. 2. The direction opposite of north.

space (sp-ay-s) [noun] 1. An open area. 2. Outside Earth's atmosphere.

speak (sp-eek) [verb] To say something with the purpose of conveying a message.

speaker (sp-ee-ker) [noun]
A device that produces or amplifies sound.
special (spesh-uhl) [adjective]
Considered to be better or greater than normal.
speech (sp-eech) [noun]
A person's way of relaying information.
speed (sp-eed) [noun], [verb]
1. The pace of which something or someone is moving.
2. To go too fast.
spell (sp-el) [verb] To write or speak the letters of a word in the proper order.
spend (sp-end) [verb] To pay for goods or services.
spider (sp-ah-yd-er) [noun]
An arachnid with eight legs and an unsegmented body.
spin (sp-in) [verb] To turn around and around at a rapid pace.
spoke (sp-ohk) [verb] The past tense of *speak*.
spoon (sp-oon) [noun]
An instrument used for eating in the form of a shallow oval on the end of a longer handle.
spot (sp-ot) [noun] A small, round area different in color or texture from its surroundings.
spread (sp-red) [verb] To apply pressure and movement in order to enlarge the surface area of something.
spring (spr-ing) [noun] The time of year after winter. 2. A coil used to give flexibility.

square (skw-ay-r) [noun]
A shape with four equal sides and four right angles.

squirrel (skw-er-uhl) [noun]
A furry, bushy-tailed rodent that lives in trees and eats nuts.

stack (st-ak) [noun] Multiple objects on top of each other.
stair (st-ayr) [noun] Multiple steps leading from one floor to another.
stand (st-and) [verb], [noun]
1. To maintain an upright position, supporting all weight on your feet. 2. A platform for holding things.
star (st-ar) [noun] 1. A point in the night sky that gives off light, similar to the sun. 2. A shape with five or six points.
start (st-art) [noun], [verb]
1. The point at which something begins. 2. To begin.
state (st-ayt) [noun]
1. The specific condition of someone or something.
2. An area of land with its own government.

station (stay-shun) [noun]
A stopping place on a public transportation route.
stay (st-ay) [verb] To remain.
stead (st-ed) [noun] A role that someone or something must fill.
steam (st-eem) [noun]
The vapor form of water.
steel (st-eel) [noun] A hard metal, usually a gray or bluish-gray color.
step (st-ep) [verb], [noun]
1. To put one foot in front of the other. 2. A small platform to help you go up to a higher place.
stick (st-ik) [noun] A small piece of wood that has fallen off of, or has been cut off of, a tree.
still (st-il) [adjective], [adverb]
1. The absence of movement.
2. Continues to be.
stone (st-ohn) [noun] A solid, non-metallic mineral matter.
stood (st-oo-d) [verb]
The past tense of *stand*.
stop (st-op) [verb] To come to an end or to prevent from moving.
store (st-ohr) [noun] A place in which goods or services are sold to the public.
storm (st-ohrm) [noun]
A disturbance of the atmosphere producing rain, lightning, thunder, snow, or high winds.

story (st-ohr-ee) [noun]
1. An account of either fact or fiction that is told for entertainment. 2. A level of a building.

straight (str-ayt) [adjective]
Extending in one direction without a curve.

strange (str-ayn-j) [adjective]
Something that is unusual or hard to understand.

straw (st-raw) [noun] A device used to drink a liquid.

stream (str-eem) [noun]
A narrow collection of flowing water.

street (str-eet) [noun] A public road.

stretch (str-ech) [verb] To make something longer or wider without tearing or breaking.

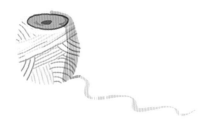

string (str-ing) [noun] Threads that can be twisted together to form a stronger material.

strong (str-awng) [adjective]
Possessing the ability to move heavy objects or remain intact despite opposition.

student (st-oo-dent) [noun]
A person who attends a school or university.

study (st-uh-dee) [verb] To commit time and attention in order to gain knowledge.

subject (sub-jekt) [noun]
A person, place, or thing that is being spoken or written about.

submarine (sub-mer-een) [noun]
A ship designed to operate completely underwater for extended periods of time.

substance (sub-stan-s) [noun]
A specific type of matter.

subtract (sub-trakt) [verb]
To take one amount away from another in order to find out the difference.

success (suk-ses) [noun]
The attaining of a goal.

sudden (sud-n) [adjective] In a short time, unexpected, and happening quickly.

suffix (suh-fix) [noun] Letters, or a letter, added to the end of a word to form a new word.

sugar (sh-oo-ger) [noun] Sweet food product formed from the sugar cane plant and processed to make a white or brown substance for sweetening food or drinks.

suggest (sug-jest) [verb]
To offer a concept, idea, or advice to another person.

suit (s-oot) [noun] Outer clothing, usually worn on more formal occasions, consisting of a top and bottom of the same material, such as a jacket and pants; jacket and skirt; or jacket, vest, and pants.

summer (suhm-er) [noun]
The time between spring and fall that includes the longest, hottest days of the year.

sun (s-uhn) [noun] The large, shining, warm circle in the sky during the day that provides Earth heat and light; a star around which the Earth and other planets in our solar system revolve.

supper (suhp-er) [noun]
A meal eaten in the evening.

supply (suhp-l-ah-y) [noun], [verb] 1. The amount available to be used. 2. To provide the required items.

support (sup-oh-rt) [verb], [noun] 1. To hold in place, to give approval, and to provide reinforcement through strength, approval, advice, or assistance. 2. A reinforcement.

sure (sh-oor) [adverb]
To be confident, reliable, trustworthy, and in agreement.

surface (ser-fis) [noun] The top or outermost layer, usually a flat or open area.

surprise (ser-pr-ah-yz) [noun]
A startling, unexpected, or unusual event.

swim (sw-im) [verb] To move through water through self-propulsion, such as fish or people in a pool.

syllable (sil-uh-bl) [noun]
The way a word is broken down into sounds; each part contains a vowel sound.

symbol (sim-buhl) [noun]
1. Something that represents something else. 2. A picture, shape, letter, or image that makes you think of something else.

system (sis-tuhm) [noun]
1. A group of rules that define a process or activity. 2. A group of objects that combine to work together or make a whole.

T

table (tay-buhl) [noun]
1. A piece of furniture made of a large, flat surface with legs to hold it up. 2. An orderly arrangement of information into rows and columns.

tablet (ta-b-lut) [noun]
An electronic device larger than a phone but typically smaller than a laptop that can often be navigated through touch.

tadpole (tad-pohl) [noun]
Baby frogs that have a rounded body with a long tail and no legs that swim and live underwater.

tail (tay-uhl) [noun] 1. The long growth from the rear of an animal's body, such as a dog's tail, a monkey's tail, or a cat's tail. 2. The rear, back, or lower part of something, such as an airplane's tail.

take (t-ayk) [verb] 1. To grasp or hold. 2. To get possession of.
talk (t-awk) [verb] To use your voice to make words.

tall (t-ah-l) [adjective] Greater than average height.

target (t-ar-g-et) [noun], [verb] 1. A mark someone is trying to hit or reach. 2. To choose as something to focus on or attack.
taste (t-ayst) [verb] To experience the flavor of food or drink.

tea (t-ee) [noun] A caffeinated beverage made by soaking tea leaves in warm water.

teach (t-eech) [verb] To help others to learn by instruction, demonstration, or interaction.
teacher (t-eech-er) [noun] Someone who teaches.
team (t-eem) [noun] A group working together for a common goal.
teeth (t-eeth) [noun] The plural of tooth.

telephone (tel-uh-fohn) [noun] A device for talking with someone at a distance by converting sound to an electrical signal and sending that signal to other telephones that convert it back to sound.
telescope (tel-uh-skohp) [noun] A magnifying device for viewing distant objects.
tell (tel) [verb] To give information or to communicate with voice or action.
temperature (temp-uh-cher) [noun] Measurement of hot or cold.

ten (ten) [noun] The whole number after nine and before eleven.

tent (t-ent) [noun] A shelter made of cloth or other material and supported by poles and ropes.

term (t-erm) [noun] 1. A word or expression with a particular meaning. 2. A particular length of time.

test (t-est) [verb], [noun] 1. To examine to find out how or whether something works or why it does not work. 2. To ask questions of someone or have them perform an activity to find their level of knowledge or skill. 3. An examination.

than (th-an) [conjunction] Used when comparing two people, places, or things.

thank (th-angk) [verb] To express appreciation.

that (th-at) [pronoun] Used in place of a particular place or thing already mentioned or indicated.

the (th-uh) [definite article] Used when talking about a person, place, or thing that is already known, is the only one, or about a singular thing that is a group.

theater (thee-uh-ter) [noun] A building where movies are played for large audiences.

their (th-ayr) [pronoun] Used to refer to *them* or *themselves*.

them (th-em) [pronoun] Another form of *they*.

then (th-en) [adverb] Immediately following or at a specific time; in the case of something.

there (th-ayr) [adverb] At a place or point in space and time or an activity.

these (th-eez) [pronoun] The plural of *this*.

they (th-ay) [pronoun] Used to refer to two or more people or things that are already spoken of or known or to refer to somebody whose gender is unknown or prefers to use the pronoun *they*.

thick (th-ik) [adjective] 1. Not thin; a large distance from one side to the other. 2. Very dense; hard to see or move through.

thin (th-in) [adjective] 1. Not thick; a very short distance from one side to the other. 2. Not dense; easy to see or move through.

thing (th-ing) [noun] A general term for referring to almost anything you can refer to: an object, a situation, a fact, a feeling, a thought, an idea, an animal, a person, etc.

think (th-ingk) [verb] To actively use your brain.

third (th-erd) [noun] 1. One of three equal parts. 2. After the first two.

this (th-i-s) [pronoun] Used to describe something already mentioned or indicated.

those (th-ohz) [pronoun] 1. The plural of *this*. 2. The people or things being referred to.

though (th-oh) [conjunction] Used when adding to what has been stated with something unlikely or different.

thought (th-awt) [noun], [verb] 1. The ideas or opinions in your mind. 2. The past tense of *think*.

thousand (th-ow-zuhnd) [noun] A large number equal to ten groups of 100; 1,000.

three (th-ree) [noun] The whole number after two and before four.

through (th-roo) [adverb] 1. From beginning to end. 2. From one side to the other.

throw (th-roh) [verb] To send something in your hand through the air with a quick motion of your arm and then release the item from your hand.

thus (th-us) [adverb] As a result of what was just said.

ticket (tik-it) [noun] A piece of paper showing payment has been made and allowing entrance to see an event, such as a movie, concert, or play, or for transportation, such as a plane ticket, train ticket, bus ticket, etc.

tie (t-ah-y) [noun] A knotted piece of clothing worn around a shirt collar, hanging down from the neck to the waistline.

tiger (t-ah-y-ger) [noun] Large, wild mammal; a member of the cat family often with black stripes.

time (t-ah-ym) [noun], [verb]
1. The measurement of the passage of seconds, minutes, hours, days, weeks, months, and years. It can be used to pinpoint when something did or will happen or how long it has been or will be until a certain event. 2. To record how long something takes.

tiny (t-ah-yn-ee) [adjective] Small, itty-bitty, or not big.

tire (t-ah-yr) [noun] A rubber ring that goes around a wheel and is inflated with air to provide a smoother ride and better grip for cars, trucks, bicycles, etc.
to (too) [adverb] Indicating the direction of movement.

toad (t-ohd) [noun] A jumping amphibian with no tail, similar to a frog, but with rough, dry, warty skin that lives on land more than in water.

toe (t-oh) [noun] One of the digits on your foot.

together (too-geth-er) [adverb] In close physical, emotional, or social contact with something or someone.
toilet (toy-lit) [noun] A large, ceramic piece of plumbing you sit on to use the bathroom.
told (t-ohld) [verb] To have given information or communicated with voice or action.

tomato (tuh-may-toh/toh-may-toh) [noun] A red, juicy fruit that is used to make ketchup.

tomorrow (tuh-mawr-oh) [noun] The day after today.
tone (t-oh-n) [noun] The quality of a sound, whether from an instrument or a voice, high or low, soft or loud, harsh or smooth, indicating a mood, feeling, or emotion.

tongue (t-ung) [noun] An organ inside your mouth that is used to taste and move food around.
too (too) [adverb] In addition or to a degree.
took (t-oo-k) [verb] The past tense of take.
tool (t-ool) [noun] A device, skill, or piece of equipment useful for completing a task.

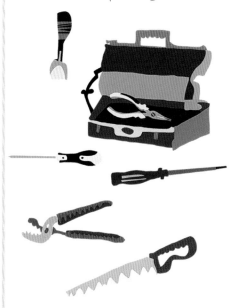

toolbox (t-ool-bok-s) [noun] A container for tools.
top (t-awp) [noun]
1. The highest part or upper surface. 2. A piece of clothing worn on the upper body.

total (toh-tl) [noun] The whole or complete amount or number.

touch (t-uch) [verb], [noun]
1. To feel something with your skin. 2. The act of feeling something with your skin.

toward (tuh-w-ord) [preposition] In the direction of something, someone, or somewhere.

town (t-own) [noun]
A community of homes, businesses, and people. Typically larger than a village but smaller than a city.

toy (t-oy) [noun] An object for children to play with.

track (tr-ak) [noun] 1. A circular path or road for racing.
2. The marks left by someone or something moving across the ground.

tractor (tr-ak-ter) [noun] A farm vehicle suitable for pulling implements or machinery around fields.

trade (tr-ayd) [verb], [noun]
1. To exchange goods or services with another person or business. 2. A person's skill or profession.

trail (tr-ay-l) [noun]
A designated outdoor path.

train (tr-ayn) [verb], [noun]
1. To teach or prepare an animal or person for an activity or sporting event. 2. Any group of vehicles, people, or animals moving in a long, narrow line. 3. A large, heavy vehicle made of several cars and an engine that travels along rails.

trapeze (trap-eez) [noun]
A horizontal bar suspended from two ropes or chains, similar to a swing, that is used for acrobatics or gymnastics.

travel (trav-uhl) [verb]
To journey from one place to another, usually somewhere far away.

treasure (trezh-er) [noun]
1. A large collection of valuables or wealth.
2. Something or someone that is highly valued.

tree (tr-ee) [noun] A tall plant with roots, a trunk, branches, and leaves that lives for decades.

triangle (trah-y-ang-guhl) [noun] A shape with three sides and three angles.

trip (tr-ip) [noun] To travel to a place and back.

trouble (tr-uh-bl) [noun] An occurrence, obstacle, event, or circumstance that causes annoyance, inconvenience, distress, or negative consequences.

truck (tr-uhk) [noun] A big, powerful vehicle for moving things.

true (tr-oo) [adjective] 1. Exactly as it is or was. 2. Agrees with the facts.

trunk (tr-ung-k) [noun]
1. The bottom of a tree.
2. A storage container in the back of a car.

try (tr-ah-y) [verb] To attempt, test, or sample.

T-shirt (tee-sh-urt) [noun] A simple piece of clothing worn over the chest shaped like the letter T.

tube (t-oob) [noun] A long, hollow channel or cylinder, usually aiding in the transport of liquids.

turkey (t-er-kee) [noun] A bird that gobbles and is often associated with Thanksgiving.

turn (t-ern) [verb] To change the direction of travel, movement, or facing by rotating to the left or right.

turnip (t-er-nip) [noun] A white root vegetable that grows underground.

turtle (t-er-t-uhl) [noun] A reptile with a hard shell that moves slowly and tucks its head in its shell when scared.

twenty (twen-tee) [noun] The whole number between nineteen and twenty-one.

twin (tw-in) [noun] Either of a pair of babies born together at the same time from the same mother.

two (too) [noun] The whole number between one and three.

type (tah-yp) [verb], [noun]
1. To write something using a keyboard. 2. Having similar character or characteristics as a group or category.

typewriter (tah-yp-rah-yt-er) [noun] A machine with keys that, when pressed, mechanically puts corresponding letters or marks on paper.

U

U.F.O. (yoo-eff-oh) [noun] Unidentified Flying Object. A vehicle or object in the sky that cannot be explained by science and is often thought to be the work of aliens.

ugly (ug-lee) [adjective] Perceived to be visually offensive, unattractive, and generally unagreeable.

ukulele (yoo-kuh-lay-lee) [noun] A musical instrument from Hawai'i similar to a small guitar.

umbrella (um-brel-uh) [noun] A shallow, dome-shaped folding frame covered in fabric with a long handle used to protect from rain or hot sunshine that collapses for easy storage.

umpire (um-pah-y-er) [noun] An official who regulates a baseball game.

uncle (ung-kl) [noun] A relative; the brother of your father or mother; the husband of your aunt or uncle.

unconscious (un-cahn-shu-s) [adjective] To not be aware of what is going on around you.

uncork (un-k-or-k) [verb] To remove a cork or other object that is stopping the flow of a liquid.

under (un-der) [adverb] Positioned beneath or below something else.

underground (un-der-gr-ow-nd) [noun], [adjective] Below the earth.

underline (un-der-lah-y-n) [verb], [noun] 1. To draw a line under words to emphasize them. 2. A line drawn under a word.

undershirt (un-der-sh-urt) [noun] A type of shirt that is typically worn underneath another piece of clothing.

understand (un-der-stand) [verb] To know, or come to know, the meaning of something or someone.

underwear (un-der-wayr) [noun] Clothing worn under the outer layer of clothes next to the skin.

undress (un-dres) [verb] To remove clothing.

unhappy (un-hap-ee) [adjective] A feeling of distress, sadness, displeasure, and disappointment.

unicorn (yoo-n-k-ohrn) [noun] A mythical, magical beast resembling a horse with a large, straight horn on its head.

unicycle (yoo-ni-sa-y-kul) [noun] A one-wheeled vehicle similar to a bike without handlebars.

uniform (yoo-nif-ohrm) [adjective], [noun] 1. All the same, without differences. 2. Matching outfits worn to show membership in a group.

unique (yoo-neek) [adjective] 1. Of particular value, quality, or nature. 2. One-of-a-kind; special.

unit (yoo-nit) [noun] 1. A standard of measurement. 2. A group or team working together that belongs to a larger group.

unite (yoo-nah-yt) [verb] To join together that which was separated or belongs together.

unkind (un-kah-ynd) [adjective] To be mean or uncaring, causing physical or emotional distress; cruel.

unlock (un-law-k) [verb] To turn a key or enter a code to disable a lock.

unmask (un-mas-sk) [verb] To remove a mask and reveal what is underneath.

unpack (un-pa-k) [verb] To take things out of a storage container.

unravel (un-ra-vul) [verb] To pull apart knitted string or yarn.

unshaven (un-shay-vun) [adjective] To not have shaved a patch of hair.

unstable (un-stay-bul) [adjective] 1. Something that is not functioning correctly. 2. Something that is close to falling over or collapsing.

untidy (un-tah-yd-ee) [adjective] To be messy, disorderly, disheveled.

until (un-til) [preposition] Up to the time stated or the given criteria having been met.

up (uhp) [noun] A direction toward the sky.

upside down (uhp-sah-yd dow-n) [adverb] Positioned so that what should be the top is at the bottom.

urgent (er-jent) [adjective] Describes when immediate action, response, or attention is required.

urn (er-n) [noun] A type of vase that is filled with something and has a lid.

us (uhs) [pronoun] Referring to the person speaking or writing and one or more others.

use (yooz) [verb] To utilize something or someone for a purpose.

useful (yoos-f-oo-l) [adjective] Something or someone that can help achieve a goal or complete a task.

useless (yoos-les) [adjective]
1. Of no use whatsoever.
2. Having no practical value.

usual (yoo-zyoo-uhl) [adjective]
1. Normal. 2. The way it is most of the time.

utensil (yoo-ten-sul) [noun] A device used to eat food, such as a fork, spoon, or knife.

V

vacant (vay-kint) [adjective] Not occupied, filled, or in use.

vaccine (va-k-see-n) [noun] A shot that helps prevent against a virus or disease.

vacuum cleaner (va-kyoo-m k-lee-ner) [noun] A device powered by electricity that picks up dirt, dust, and debris.

valley (val-ee) [noun] A lowland between two mountains, often with a river running through it.

value (val-yoo) [noun] The usefulness, price, or worth of something or someone.

vampire (vam-pah-y-r) [noun] A mythical creature that often has sharp fangs and pale skin.

van (v-an) [noun] A vehicle larger and taller than a car with a box-like interior for carrying people or cargo.

vanish (van-ish) [verb] To disappear or pass from sight quickly and without obvious explanation.

varnish (vahr-nish) [noun] A transparent, paint-like liquid that, when applied and dried, leaves a see-through, hard, shiny surface.

vary (vay-ree) [verb] To have or make small changes in several similar things over time.

vase (vay-s) [noun] A decorative container used to hold cut flowers.

vegetable (vej-tuh-buhl) [noun] The edible part of a plant.

vehicle (vee-hi-kuhl) [noun] A wheeled machine used to transport goods, people, etc.

vein (vay-n) [noun] 1. A blood vessel through which blood flows toward the heart.
2. Similar pathways or flows.

vending machine (ven-ding muh-shee-n) [noun] A device that dispenses items to users after someone puts money into the machine and picks what they want.

Venus (vee-nus) [noun]
The second planet from the sun in our solar system.
verb (v-erb) [noun] A word that describes action or experience.
verse (v-ers) [noun] 1. Writing in which the words rhyme or follow a beat. 2. A portion of a song.
vest (v-est) [noun] A sleeveless piece of outerwear worn on the chest.

vet (v-et) [noun] 1. An animal doctor (short for veterinarian). 2. A person with substantial previous experience, particularly in the military.
victory (vik-tohr-ee) [noun] Success in achieving a goal, overcoming an obstacle, or winning against an enemy.
video (vi-dee-oh) [noun] A series of moving pictures.

videographer (vi-dee-aw-grah-fur) [noun] A person who makes videos.
view (v-yoo) [noun] 1. All that can be seen from a certain point. 2. An opinion.

village (vil-ij) [noun] A small community, smaller than a town.
villain (vil-in) [noun] 1. The bad guy in a story or real life. 2. A mean, deceitful, or evil person.

violin (vah-yuh-lin) [noun] A small, stringed musical instrument played with a bow.
visit (viz-it) [noun] To go to see another place, or person, for a brief stay.
visor (va-y-zer) [noun] A hat that does not cover the top of the head.
vitamin (vah-yt-uh-min) [noun] Substance or chemical that is good or vital to the health of a living thing, either in pill form or occurring in food that is eaten.
voice (voy-s) [noun] The sound made by a person with their vocal chords.

volcano (vawl-kay-noh) [noun] A mountain formed at a vent in the Earth's crust from molten rock or lava coming up from deep inside the Earth.

volleyball (v-awl-ee-bawl) [noun] A sport played between two teams by hitting a ball back and forth over a net.

volt (v-ohl-t) [noun] A unit of electric force.

volume (v-awl-yoo-m) [noun] 1. How loud something is. 2. Amount of space occupied in a container.
vow (v-ow) [noun] An oath or solemn promise.

vowel (v-ow-uhl) [noun] A particular type of letter. The English vowels are a, e, i, o, u, and sometimes y.
voyage (voy-ij) [noun] A journey in a ship or by water.

W

waffle (w-aw-f-uhl) [noun] A distinct breakfast pastry with crevices, often eaten with syrup.

wagon (wa-ee-gin) [noun] A four-wheeled cart of rectangular shape for carrying people or cargo that is usually pulled.

waist (way-st) [noun] 1. The narrow part of the human body above the hips and below the chest. 2. The part of an article of clothing that fits this part of the body.

wait (wayt) [verb] To remain in place, or not do something, in anticipation of some event yet to happen.

walk (wahk) [verb] To travel by foot.

walking stick (wahk-ing stik) [noun] A stick used to help somebody walk.

wall (w-ahl) [noun] A structure, usually strong and solid, that divides one area from another, sometimes supporting a roof.

wallet (w-awl-et) [noun] An object to hold money and cards that is often kept in a pocket or purse.

wand (w-ah-nd) [noun] 1. A prop used by magicians to help with their magic tricks. 2. A fantastical, thin stick that performs magic.

want (w-ah-nt) [verb], [noun] 1. To desire something. 2. Something needed or desired.

warm (w-ohm) [adjective] Mildly hotter than the surroundings, usually in a comfortable way.

warn (w-ohrn) [verb] To advise that something unwanted or dangerous may or will happen, particularly so that it can be prevented or avoided.

was (wuz) [verb] The past tense of *be*.

wash (w-ah-sh) [verb] To make clean.

wasp (w-ah-sp) [noun] A flying insect that is known to sting when provoked.

watch (w-ah-ch) [noun], [verb] 1. A piece of jewelry that indicates the time. 2. To observe or look at with attention.

water (w-aht-er) [noun] A liquid made of oxygen and hydrogen that is tasteless, colorless, and odorless in its pure form. It falls as rain and is what makes the rivers, streams, lakes, and oceans of the world. It is essential to life as we know it.

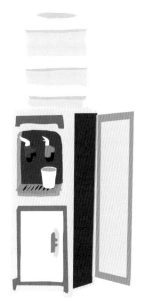

water cooler (w-aht-er k-oo-ler) [noun] A container for water that can be turned on and off to let water come out.

watermelon (w-aht-er-m-el-un) [noun] A round, striped, green fruit with red pulp and black seeds.

wave (way-v) [noun], [verb]
1. A swell in the surface of water that moves.
2. To make any wave-like motion.
way (w-ay) [noun]
1. The method in which something is done or accomplished. 2. The path or track followed to get somewhere.
we (w-ee) [pronoun] Used by the person speaking to refer to themself and another or others.
wear (w-ayr) [verb] 1. To use as clothing. 2. To become eroded, weaker, or thinner from usage or over time.

weather (weth-er) [noun]
The way it is outside: hot, cold, raining, sunny, windy, etc.

web (w-eb) [noun] 1. A sticky substance made by spiders. 2. Another name for the Internet.

website (w-eb-sah-y-t) [noun] Somewhere you can visit online with parental permission, such as www.flowerpotpress.com.
weed (w-eed) [noun]
An undesirable, unwanted plant in a garden or lawn.
week (w-eek) [noun]
Seven days in a row.
weight (wayt) [noun]
A measurement of the force of gravity on an object.

welcome mat (w-el-k-um m-at) [noun] A decorative object put outside of doors for visitors to wipe their shoes on before entering a home.
well (w-el) [noun] 1. A deep hole, drilled or dug in the ground, to get water.
2. A feeling of good health.
went (w-ent) [verb] 1. The past tense of *go*. 2. To have moved or traveled away from or to a particular place.
were (w-er) [verb] The past tense of *be*.
west (w-est) [noun] 1. One of the four cardinal directions.
2. The direction the sun sets.

wetsuit (w-et-s-oot) [noun] A piece of clothing worn over the whole body to help you move in water and protect your skin.
whale (w-ay-l) [noun] A large mammal that lives underwater.
what (wut) [adverb] Used to question a person, place, or thing.

103

wheel (w-eel) [noun] A circular object that spins around its center point.

wheelchair (w-eel-ch-ay-r) [noun] A wheeled device that helps people move around.

when (w-en) [adverb] Used to specify at what time a certain event will occur.

where (wayr) [adverb] Used to talk about a place in space or time.

whether (weth-er) [conjunction] 1. Used to speak of two or more options, only one of which can occur. 2. To say that something will or won't happen no matter the situation.

which (w-ich) [pronoun] Used when uncertain about who or what people or things in a group are being referred to.

while (wah-yl) [conjunction] During the time that something is happening.

whisper (wis-per) [noun], [verb] 1. Something spoken very quietly and softly. 2. To speak very quietly.

white (wah-yt) [noun] 1. The color of fresh snow, milk, or sugar. 2. All the wavelengths of the visible spectrum of light.

who (hoo) [pronoun] Used to talk or ask about a person or ask the name of a person.

whole (h-ohl) [adjective] 1. The complete thing. 2. All of something.

whose (hooz) [pronoun] Belonging to or relating to the person spoken of, or question the ownership of something.

why (w-ahy) [adverb] Used to ask about the reason or cause.

wide (w-ahyd) [adjective] The distance from side-to-side, or across, measured at right angles to the length.

wife (w-ahyf) [noun] A married woman.

wig (w-ig) [noun] Artificial hair worn on the head.

wild (wah-yld) [adjective] Living in its natural state, out of human control.

will (w-il) [noun] Determination to achieve a goal.

win (w-in) [verb] To be first, the most successful, or the person selected in a competition.

wind (w-ind) [noun] Air that is moving.

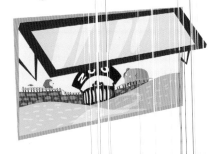

window (win-doh) [noun] An opening in a wall, usually covered with glass, that lets in light.

wing (w-ing) [noun] 1. The part of a bird, bat, or bug's body that is used to fly. 2. The parts of a plane that stick out the sides that allows it to fly.

wink (w-ing-k) [verb] To close one eye to let someone know you understand.

winter (win-ter) [noun] The season between fall and spring, usually with the coldest, shortest days of the year.

wire (wah-yr) [noun] Long, flexible lengths of metal, usually covered in plastic or rubber.

wish (w-ish) [verb], [noun] 1. To want or desire very much for something to happen or be true. 2. The thing you want to happen.

witch (w-ich) [noun]
A fantastical character who performs magic and makes potions.

with (w-ith) [preposition]
Referring to two or more things together, or one possessing or accompanying the other.

wizard (w-iz-urd) [noun]
A fantastical person who performs magic and makes potions.

woman (w-oo-muhn) [noun]
An adult female human.

women (wim-in) [noun]
More than one woman.

wonder (wuhn-der) [verb], [noun] 1. To ponder or think about a question and its possible answers. 2. A feeling of admiration, surprise, and awe at something impressive, unexpected, or beautiful.

wood (w-oo-d) [noun]
1. The material that makes up the interior of trees. 2. An area smaller than a forest with many trees growing there.

wool (w-oo-l) [noun]
1. The soft, thick hair of sheep. 2. The material made from shearing a sheep.

word (w-erd) [noun]
The smallest unit of spoken language that carries a meaning.

work (w-erk) [verb], [noun]
1. To do the activities, tasks, or duties of your job.
2. To exert effort to do a task.
3. What you do or where you go for a job.

worker (w-ur-ker) [noun]
Someone who has a job.

world (w-erld) [noun] Referring to the Earth, or other planets, or the realm where someone exists.

would (w-oo-d) [verb] Used when speaking of past imagined, requested, or desired situations.

wrench (ren-ch) [noun] A hand tool used to tighten or loosen nuts and bolts.

write (rah-yt) [verb] To form letters and words with a pen, pencil, or keyboard.

written (rit-uhn) [adjective]
Recorded in writing.

wrong (rong) [adjective]
To be incorrect, unjust, unfair, not satisfactory.

wrote (r-oht) [verb] The past tense of *write*.

X

x-ray (eks-ray) [noun]
1. A very short wavelength form of electromagnetic radiation.
2. Photographs taken using x-rays that show a person's bones. They are used by doctors to diagnose problems such as broken bones.

xylophone (x-ah-y-luh-fohn) [noun] A musical instrument made of bars of wood or metal of varying lengths that are struck with mallets to create musical notes.

A B C D E F G H I J K L M N O P Q R S T U V W X Y Z

Y

yacht (yawt) [noun] A boat, sailboat, or motorboat that is of a superior quality for personal use, racing, or pleasure cruising, as opposed to a working boat that carries cargo or paying passengers.

yak (y-ak) [noun] A large, usually wild, variety of ox. They have long, shaggy hair and are from the highlands of Tibet.

yard (y-awrd) [noun] 1. A unit of measurement equal to three feet. 2. The land surrounding a building.

yarn (y-arn) [noun] A material used to knit things.

yawn (y-awn) [noun] A deep breath when opening the mouth very wide to deliver extra oxygen to your brain, especially when tired.

year (y-eer) [noun] 1. A measure of time equal to the time taken for the Earth to make one full orbit of the sun. 2. Twelve months.

yellow (yel-oh) [noun] A primary color. The color of the sun, ripe lemons, butter, and bananas.

yes (yes) [interjection] Used to express agreement, approval, or assent.

yesterday (yes-ter-day) [noun] The day before today.

yet (yet) [adverb] At the present time, up to a particular time, or in the time remaining.

yoga (yoh-guh) [noun] 1. A Hindu philosophy of mind and body control and introspection. 2. A series of breathing, posing, and stretching exercises designed to unify mind and body for peace and tranquility.

yogurt (yoh-gert) [noun] A food made by adding particular bacteria to milk, often including the addition of sweeteners and flavoring.

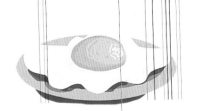

yolk (yohk) [noun] The yellow center of an egg.

you (yoo) [pronoun] Used to refer to the person being spoken to.

young (yung) [adjective] In the early stages of life.

your (yohr) [pronoun] Used when referring to you or yourself.

youth (yoo-th) [noun] The time of life when someone is young, or the characteristics of being young.

yo-yo (yoh-yoh) [noun], [verb] 1. A toy on a string that goes up and down. 2. To play with a yo-yo.

Z

zebra (zee-bruh) [noun] A horse-like mammal, native to Africa, known for its white and dark-brown or black stripes.

zeppelin (zep-uh-lin) [noun] A type of flying aircraft.

zero (zee-roh) [noun] 1. A number meaning none or nothing. 2. The symbol 0, or zero, means there is no negative or starting value. 3. It is the starting point from which you measure or count.

zigzag (zig-zag) [noun], [adjective] A series, or pattern, of short, sharp turns.

zipper (zip-er) [noun] A closure device or fastener used on clothing consisting of two rows of plastic or metal teeth and a piece that slides between them to open or close the zipper by pulling the rows together or apart.

zoo (zoo) [noun] A park with areas, or enclosures, confining animals where they are on display for people to see.
zoom (zoo-m) [verb] 1. To go very fast. 2. To change the distance at which you are looking at an object, such as with a magnifying glass.

zucchini (zoo-kee-nee) [noun] A large green fruit similar to a cucumber.

Zzz (zee-zee-zee/zee-z) [noun] A symbol representing sleeping or snoring that is often used in cartoons and comics.